Knits

FOR YOU AND YOUR HOME

Photography by Penny Wincer

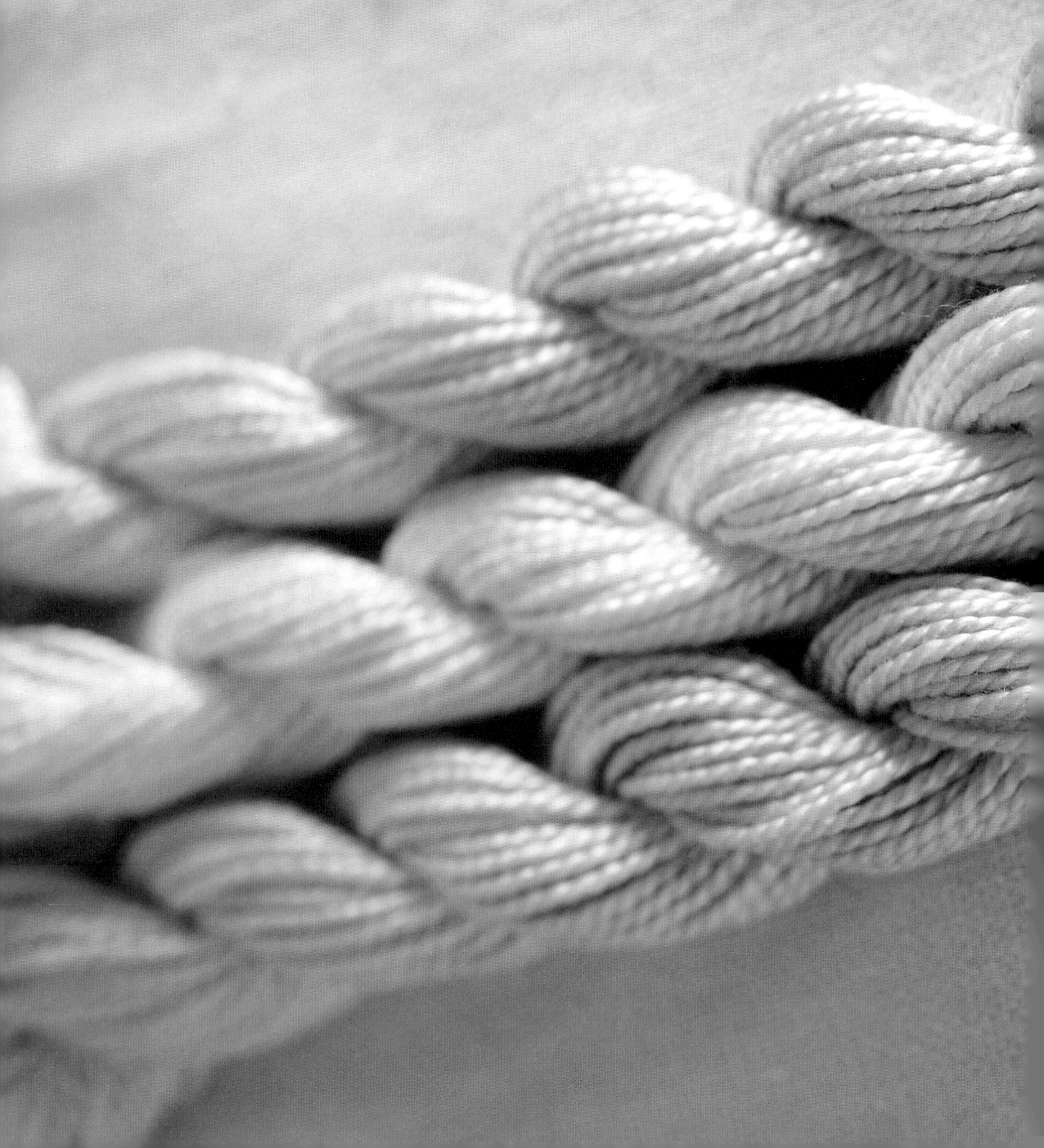

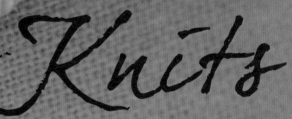

Knits

FOR YOU AND
YOUR HOME

30 BLISSFUL KNITS TO INDULGE,
COCOON, PAMPER AND DETOX

T

TRAFALGAR SQUARE
North Pomfret, Vermont

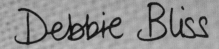

Debbie Bliss

Contents

In a world where everything is "on the go" and there seems to be a constant pressure to be everything to everyone, the everyday stresses of life can make it difficult to allow time for ourselves.

Whenever I meet knitters I am reminded time and time again that they are some of the most selfless of people; so many times I hear "I am making this project for a friend/partner/grandchild" or the classic "I never have time to make anything for myself." So with this book of thirty designs I hope to entice the crafter—if only for a short time—away from the projects they are planning to make for everyone else and to knit something for themselves. (Although should it be admired, of course, there is no reason why it can't join the list of knits to make for others!)

I have divided the book into four sections—Indulge, Cocoon, Pamper, and Detox and each contains a mix of knits to wear as well as projects to help decorate and organize your home.

Indulge has projects to make you feel that little bit extra-special, bringing some well-deserved glamour into your life. Get some movie-queen style with delicate knits in super-fine, gossamer-like mohair, a 1920's style turban for your inner flapper, and a beautiful classic beaded purse.

Pamper is for the ultimate time out, so bring the spa into your home and put your feet up on a giant pouf, drift off with a sleep mask or make hearts containing relaxing lavender. While for those of you who, like me, suffer from "knitter's neck" there is a neck pillow that can be heated up for extra soothing powers.

Detox, is for those who sometimes relax by puttering around. I relax by sorting out my crayons by color or my sketchbooks by size, rearranging my mood boards, gently tidying (but nothing too energetic!), so in this section I have included projects that will help you to sort, stack, and tuck away.

Cocoon has knits to wrap around and comfort you, from super-soft throws and a snuggly snood to cozy chair covers. The designs to wear are in luxurious fibers, which are ever so gentle against your skin.

Many of the projects are quick to make or use only a single ball, so go on, take some time out for yourself—you are worth it.

This book would not have been possible without the invaluable help of Rosy Tucker who came up with the wonderful home projects while I concentrated on the wearables. We hope you enjoy the book.

Debbie Bliss

Types of Yarn

The yarns I have chosen for the designs in this book range from my organic cotton to cashmerinos and pure wools, each with their own contribution to make to the designs. It may be that they give crisp stitch detail in a simple pattern, such as the accessories holder worked in cotton (right and page 82), or provide softness and elegance in a shrug (page 130).

Unless you are using up your stash to make the smaller items in this book, make the effort to buy the yarn stated in the pattern. Each of these designs has been created with a specific yarn in mind.

A different yarn may not produce the same quality of fabric or have the same wash and wear properties. From an aesthetic point of view, the clarity of a subtle stitch pattern may be lost if a project is knitted in an inferior yarn. However, there may be occasions when a knitter needs to substitute a yarn—if there is an allergy to wool, for example—and so the following is a guide to making the most informed choices.

Always buy a yarn that is the same weight as the one given in the pattern: replace a double knitting with a double knitting, for example, and check that the recommended gauge of both yarns is the same.

Where you are substituting a different fiber, be aware of the design. A cable pattern knitted in cotton when worked in wool will pull in because of the greater elasticity of the yarn and so the fabric will become narrower; this will alter the proportions of the knitting.

Check the yardage of the yarn. Yarns that weigh the same may have different lengths in the ball or hank, so you may need to buy more or less yarn.

The following are descriptions of my yarns used in this book and a guide to their weights and types (see page 10).

Debbie Bliss Andes:

* A double-knitting-weight yarn.

* 65% baby alpaca, 35% mulberry silk.

* Approximately 110yd (100m)/1¾oz (50g) hank.

Debbie Bliss Angel:

* A lightweight mohair-blend yarn.

* 76% superkid mohair, 24% silk.

* Approximately 218yd (200m)/⅞oz (25g) ball.

Debbie Bliss Baby Cashmerino:

* A fine-weight yarn.

* 55% merino wool, 33% microfiber, 12% cashmere.

* Approximately 137yd (125m)/1¾oz (50g) ball.

Debbie Bliss Cashmerino Aran:

* An aran-weight yarn.

* 55% merino wool, 33% microfiber, 12% cashmere.

* Approximately 99yd (90m)/1¾oz (50g) ball.

Debbie Bliss Cashmerino DK:

* A double-knitting-weight yarn.

* 55% merino wool, 33% microfiber, 12% cashmere.

* Approximately 120yd (110m)/1¾oz (50g) ball.

Debbie Bliss Cotton DK:

* A double-knitting-weight yarn.

* 100% cotton.

* Approximately 92yd (84m)/1¾oz (50g) ball.

Debbie Bliss Eco Baby:

* A fine-weight yarn.

* 100% organic cotton.

* Approximately 137yd (125m)/ 1¾oz (50g) ball.

Debbie Bliss Paloma:

* A bulky-weight yarn.

* 60% baby alpaca, 40% merino wool.

* Approximately 71yd (65m)/1¾oz (50g) ball.

Debbie Bliss Rialto Aran:

* An aran-weight yarn.

* 100% extra-fine merino wool.

* Approximately 88yd (80m)/1¾oz (50g) ball.

Debbie Bliss Rialto Chunky:

* A bulky-weight yarn.

* 100% merino wool.

* Approximately 66yd (60m)/1¾oz (50g) ball.

Debbie Bliss Rialto 4-Ply:

* A super-fine-weight yarn.

* 100% extra fine merino wool.

* Approximately 197yd (180m)/1¾oz (50g) ball.

Debbie Bliss Rialto Lace:

* A lace-weight yarn.

* 100% extra fine merino wool.

* Approximately 427yd (390m)/1¾oz (50g) ball.

Buying yarn

The yarn label on the yarn will carry all the essential information you need as to gauge, needle size, weight, and yardage. Importantly, it will also have the dye-lot number. Yarns are dyed in batches or lots, which can vary considerably. As your retailer may not have the same dye lot later on, buy all your yarn for a project at the same time. If you know that sometimes you use more yarn than that quoted in the pattern, buy extra. If it is not possible to buy all the yarn you need with the same dye-lot number, use the different ones where it will not show as much, on a neck or border, as a change of dye lot across a main piece will most likely show.

It is also a good idea at the time of buying the yarn that you check the pattern and make sure that you already have the needles you will require. If not buy them now, as it will save a lot of frustration when you get home.

Abbreviations

The abbreviations on the next page are standard ones. Any special abbreviations needed are provided at the beginning of the individual patterns.

STANDARD ABBREVIATIONS

alt	alternate
beg	begin(ning)
cm	centimeter(s)
cont	continu(e)(ing)
dec	decreas(e)(ing)
foll	follow(s)(ing)
g	gram(s)
in	inch(es)
inc	increas(e)(ing)
k	knit
kfb	knit into front and back of next stitch
m	meter(s)
mm	millimeter(s)
M1	make one stitch by picking up the loop lying between the stitch just worked and the next stitch and working into the back of it
oz	ounce(s)
p	purl
patt	pattern; or work in pattern
psso	pass slipped stitch over
rem	remain(s)(ing)
rep	repeat(s)(ing)
skpo	slip 1, knit 1, pass slipped stitch over
sl	slip
ssk	[slip 1 knitwise] twice, insert tip of left-hand needle from left to right through fronts of slipped stitches and k2tog
st(s)	stitch(es)
St st	stockinette stitch
tbl	through back loop(s)
tog	together
yd	yard(s)
yo	yarn over right needle to make a new stitch

Pamper

Bath Bag

This bag is perfect for keeping all your bathroom accessories in. Hang it on the back of your bathroom door to ensure it is always at hand and fill with all your special pampering products. No longer will you have to scrabble around trying to find your bathroom treats; you can feel organized and relaxed. Knitted in a classic combination of ecru and stone and lined with an attractive spotty fabric, this easily transportable bath bag will suit every bathroom.

SIZE

Approximately 25¼in/63cm in circumference x 11in/28cm tall (from base).

MATERIALS

* ✳ Six 1¾ oz (50g) balls of Debbie Bliss Cotton DK in Ecru 02 (A) and four balls in Stone 19 (B)
* ✳ Pair of size 9 (5.5mm) knitting needles
* ✳ Piece of cardboard, 10¾in x 6in/27cm x 15cm
* ✳ 12½in/32cm of lining fabric, 36in/90cm wide
* ✳ Sewing thread

GAUGE

16 sts and 24 rows to 4in/10cm square over patt using size 9 (5.5mm) needles and two strands of yarn used together.

ABBREVIATIONS

pkp = [purl, knit, purl] all into next st. Also see page 11.

NOTE
The bag is made in one piece.

TO MAKE
Bag base
With size 9 (5.5mm) needles and two strands of B used together, cast on 29 sts.

1st row (right side) K1, [p1, k1] to end.

2nd row K1, pkp, [k1, p1] 5 times, k1, [pkp, k1] twice, [p1, k1] 5 times, pkp, k1. **37 sts.**

3rd row Rep 1st row.

4th row [K1, pkp] twice, [k1, p1] 5 times, k1, [pkp, k1] 4 times, [p1, k1] 5 times, [pkp, k1] twice. **53 sts.**

5th row Rep 1st row.

6th row [K1, pkp] twice, [k1, p1] 9 times, k1, [pkp, k1] 4 times, [p1, k1] 9 times, [pkp, k1] twice. **69 sts.**

7th and 8th rows [Rep 1st row] twice.

9th row [K1, pkp] twice, [k1, p1] 13 times, k1, [pkp, k1] 4 times, [p1, k1] 13 times, [pkp, k1] twice. **85 sts.**

10th, 11th, and 12th rows [Rep 1st row] 3 times.

13th row [K1, pkp] twice, [k1, p1] 17 times, k1, [pkp, k1] 4 times, [p1, k1] 17 times, [pkp, k1] twice. **101 sts.**

14th and 15th rows [Rep 1st row] twice.

1st ridge row (wrong side) K all sts.

2nd ridge row (right side) P all sts.

Main bag
Change to two strands of A used together and work in patt as follows:

1st row (wrong side) Purl.

2nd row P2, [k1, p3] to last 3 sts, k1, p2.

3rd row Purl.

4th row K1, [p3, k1] to end.

These 4 rows **form** the main patt and are repeated until work measures 10in/25cm from 2nd ridge row, ending with a 2nd or 4th row.

Change to two strands of B used together and beg with a p row, cont in patt for 6 rows more.

Bind off knitwise on wrong side.

STRAPS (make 2)
With size 9 (5.5mm) needles and two strands of B used together, cast on 5 sts.

Seed st row K1, [p1, k1] twice.

Rep last row until strap measures approximately 18in/46cm.

Bind off in seed st.

TO FINISH
Fold cast on edge in half and join base seam to ridge rows, then continue to join the side seam to cast off edge.

Lining
Cut a cardboard oval shape for the base, approximately 6in x 10¾in/15cm x 27cm. Use the cardboard shape to cut a base from lining, adding ⅝in/ 1.5cm all around for seams. Cut a fabric rectangle approximately 12½in x 29¼in/32cm x 74cm, then with right sides together, sew the short ends together to form a tube, taking a ½in/1cm seam. Stitch the lining base into the tube. Position the straps equally spaced on each side of the bag and stitch in place to the outside of the bag. Place the cardboard base in the bag, then slipstitch the lining into the bag around the top edge, turning the excess fabric onto the wrong side and matching the seam in the lining to the seam in the bag.

Lavender Hearts

These pretty and delicious smelling hanging hearts take just a single ball of Baby Cashmerino to make, plus some inexpensive silver embroidery beads for added sparkle. Although the beading makes these hearts look complicated, they are in fact deceptively simple to make as each bead is threaded onto the yarn before being worked into the knitted fabric. The patterned backing fabric takes this sophisticated design a step further by allowing you to add your own personality to each heart.

SIZE
Approximately 3½in x 3½in/9cm x 9cm.

MATERIALS
* One 1¾ oz (50g) ball of Debbie Bliss Baby Cashmerino in Silver 012
* Pair of size 3 (3.25mm) knitting needles.
* 82 small glass embroidery beads per heart—silver lined clear glass beads, size SB07 color 1
* Piece of backing fabric, 5in/13cm square, for each heart
* Lengths of ribbon, ⅛in/3mm wide
* Dried lavender flowers
* Optional lavender essential oil to enhance the aroma or freshen old lavender

GAUGE
25 sts and 34 rows to 4in/10cm square over St st using size 3 (3.25mm) needles.

ABBREVIATIONS
PB = bring yarn to front of work, slip 1 st, push bead along the yarn close to the work, take the yarn to back of work. Also see page 11.

BEADING NOTE

* Before casting on, you need to thread the beads onto the yarn. If your beading needle is made from very fine wire with a long collapsible eye, you can thread the beads directly onto the yarn. If you have to use a fine needle with a small eye, you need to thread the needle with a length of sewing thread tied to form a loop, then thread the yarn through the loop, so the beads thread onto the sewing thread first, then onto the yarn.

* The beads need to have a center hole large enough for two thicknesses of yarn to pass through, or you will not be able to thread the beads. You may find a few beads that have a slightly smaller center hole, this is due to a thicker than normal coating of silver and you will need to discard these but one 15g tube of the specified beads should be sufficient for three hearts.

TO MAKE

With size 3 (3.25mm) needles, cast on 3 sts.
1st and every foll wrong-side row Purl.
2nd row K1, [M1, k1] twice. **5 sts.**
4th row K1, M1, k1, p1, k1, M1, k1. **7 sts.**
6th row K1, M1, k2, PB, k2, M1, k1. **9 sts.**
8th row K1, M1, k1, PB, k3, B1, k1, M1, k1. **11 sts.**
10th row K1, M1, PB, [k3, PB] twice, M1, k1. **13 sts.**
12th row K1, M1, k3, [PB, k3] twice, M1, k1. **15 sts.**
14th row K1, M1, k2, [PB, k3] twice, PB, k2, M1, k1. **17 sts.**
16th row K1, M1, k1, [PB, k3] 3 times, PB, k1, M1, k1. **19 sts.**
18th row K1, M1, [PB, k3] 4 times, PB, M1, k1. **21 sts.**
20th row K4, [PB, k3] 4 times, k1.
22nd row K1, M1, k1, [PB, k3] 4 times, PB, k1, M1, k1. **23 sts.**
24th row K1, [PB, k3] 5 times, PB, k1.
26th row K1, M1, k2, [PB, k3] 4 times, PB, k2, M1, k1. **25 sts.**
28th row K2, [PB, k3] 5 times, PB, k2.
30th row K1, M1, k3, [PB, k3] 5 times, M1, k1. **27 sts.**
32nd row K3, [PB, k3] 6 times.
34th row K1, [PB, k3] 6 times, PB, k1.
36th row K3, [PB, k3] 6 times.
37th row P to end.

Shape top of first side

38th row (right side) K1, [PB, k3] 3 times, turn and leave rem 14 sts on a holder.
39th row P2tog, p to end. **12 sts.**
40th row K2tog tbl, k1, [PB, k3] twice, k1. **11 sts.**
41st row P2tog, p to end. **10 sts.**
42nd row K2tog tbl, k2, PB, k5. **9 sts.**
43rd row P2tog, p to last 2 sts, p2tog tbl. **8 sts.**
44th row K2tog tbl, k4, k2tog. **6 sts.**
Bind-off row P2tog, [p1, pass 1st st over 2nd st] twice, p2tog tbl, pass 1st st over 2nd st, fasten off last st.

Shape top of second side

38th row With right side facing, join yarn to rem 14 sts on holder, k2tog tbl, k2, [PB, k3] twice, PB, k1. **13 sts.**
39th row P1, p to last 2 sts, p2tog tbl. **12 sts.**
40th row K4, PB, k3, PB, k1, k2tog. **11 sts.**
41st row P to last 2 sts, p2tog tbl. **10 sts.**
42nd row K5, PB, k2, k2tog. **9 sts.**
43rd row P to last 2 sts, p2tog tbl. **8 sts.**
44th row K2tog tbl, k4, k2tog. **6 sts.**
Bind-off row P2tog, [p1, pass 1st st over 2nd st] twice, p2tog tbl, pass 1st st over 2nd st and fasten off.

TO FINISH

Using the knitted heart as a template, cut a piece of fabric the same shape, adding ³/₈in/5mm all around the edge. Lay knitted heart on fabric heart with right sides together and carefully stitch around the edge, leaving an opening along one side. Clip the fabric around the curved edges and turn right side out. Cut a length of ribbon and tie the two ends together securely and fold at the center (opposite the knot). Thread the ribbon fold into a large-eyed needle and working through the gap in the seam, pass the needle with the ribbon through the V of the heart; this forms a hanging loop with the knot holding it in place inside the heart. Fold the seam allowance along the opening onto the wrong side, fill the heart with lavender, and sew the opening closed.

Cape Coat

This luxury coat is perfect for all occasions—whether you wear it while lounging around your home, taking your children to school, meeting friends, or whilst doing all three, you will feel comfortable and look stylish. I have made this warming coat in a neutral beige to ensure it goes with every outfit and eventuality, but if you prefer, make it a statement piece by knitting it in a more striking color. This classically designed simple cape coat will look wonderful in any shade.

MEASUREMENTS

To fit bust

32–34	36–38	40–42	in
81–86	92–97	102–107	cm

Finished measurements

Width

39 1/2	43 3/4	48 1/2	in
100	111	123	cm

Length to shoulder

30 1/4	31 1/2	33	in
77	80	84	cm

MATERIALS

* 20(22:24) 1 3/4 oz (50g) balls of Debbie Bliss Cashmerino DK in Beige 43
* One size 6 (4mm) circular knitting needle
* Pair of size 3 (3.25mm) knitting needles
* One large button

GAUGE

26 sts and 30 rows to 4in/10cm square over patt using size 6 (4mm) needles.

ABBREVIATIONS

See page 11.

BACK

With size 6 (4mm) circular needle, cast on 210(234:258) sts.

Work backward and forward in rows.

1st row (right side) P2, [k2, p2] to end.

2nd row K2, [p2, k2] to end.

These 2 rows **form** the rib and are repeated.

Work 3 rows more in rib.

Inc row (wrong side) K2, [p1, M1, p1, k2] to end. **262(292:322) sts.**

Now work in patt as follows:

1st row P2, [sl 1, k2, psso, p2] to end.

2nd row K2, [p1, yo, p1, k2] to end.

3rd row P2, [k3, p2] to end.

4th row K2, [p3, k2] to end.

These 4 rows **form** the patt and are repeated.

Cont in patt until back measures 20(20½:21)in/51(52:53)cm from cast-on edge, ending with a wrong-side row.

Shape upper arms

Bind off 2 sts at beg of next 78(86:94) rows. **106(120:134) sts.**

Shape shoulders

Bind off 11(13:15) sts at beg of next 4 rows and 11(12:13) sts at beg of foll 2 rows. **40(44:48) sts.**

Bind off.

LEFT FRONT

With size 6 (4mm) circular needle, cast on 112(124:136) sts.

Work backward and forward in rows.

1st row (right side) [P2, k2] to last 8 sts, k8.

2nd row K8, [p2, k2] to end.

These 2 rows **form** the rib with garter st front edge and are repeated.

Work 3 rows more in rib as set.

Inc row (wrong side) K8, [p1, M1, p1, k2] to end. **138(153:168) sts.**

Now work in patt as follows:

1st row [P2, sl 1, k2, psso] to last 8 sts, k8.

2nd row K8, [p1, yo, p1, k2] to end.

3rd row [P2, k3] to last 8 sts, k8.

4th row K8, [p3, k2] to end.

These 4 rows **form** the patt with garter st front edge and are repeated.

Cont in patt until front measures 20(20½:21)in/51(52:53)cm from cast-on edge, ending with a wrong-side row.

Shape upper arm

Bind off 2 sts at beg of next row and 29(33:37) foll right-side rows. **78(85:92) sts.**

Next row Patt to end.

Shape neck

Next row Bind off 2 sts, patt to last 11(13:15) sts, leave these 11(13:15) sts on a holder, turn and work on rem sts. **65(70:75) sts.**

Next row Bind off 2 sts, patt to end.

Next row Bind off 2 sts, patt to end.

Rep the last 2 rows 7 times more.

Next row Patt to end. **33(38:43) sts.**

Shape shoulder

Bind off 11(13:15) sts at beg of next row and foll right-side row.

Work 1 row.

Bind off rem 11(12:13) sts.

RIGHT FRONT

With size 6 (4mm) circular needle, cast on 112(124:136) sts.

Work backward and forward in rows.

1st row (right side) K8, [k2, p2] to end.

2nd row [K2, p2] to last 8 sts, k8.

These 2 rows **form** the rib with garter st front edge and are repeated.

Work 3 rows more in rib as set.

Inc row [K2, p1, M1, p1] to last 8 sts, k8. **138(153:168) sts.**

Now work in patt as follows:

1st row K8, [sl 1, k2, psso, p2] to end.

2nd row [K2, p1, yo, p1] to last 8 sts, k8.

3rd row K8, [k3, p2] to end.

4th row [K2, p3] to last 8 sts, k8.

These 4 rows **form** the patt with garter st edge and are repeated.

Cont in patt until front measures 20(20½:21)in/51(52:53)cm from cast-on edge, ending with a right-side row.

Shape upper arm

Bind off 2 sts at beg of next row and 30(34:38) foll wrong-side rows. **76(83:90) sts.**

Shape neck

Next row Patt 11(13:15) sts, leave these 11(13:15) sts on a holder, patt to end. **65(70:75) sts**

Next row Bind off 2 sts, patt to end.

Next row Bind off 2 sts, patt to end.

Rep the last 2 rows 7 times more. **33(38:43) sts.**

Shape shoulder

Bind off 11(13:15) sts at beg of next row and foll right-side row.

Work 1 row.

Bind off rem 11(12:13) sts.

NECKBAND

Sew shoulder and upper arm seams.

With size 3 (3.25mm) needles, slip 11(13:15) sts from right front holder onto a needle, pick up and k 22 sts up right front neck, 40(44:48) sts from back neck, 22 sts down left front neck, then patt 11(13:15) sts from left front holder. **106(114:122) sts.**

K 5 rows.

Buttonhole row K4, k2tog, yo2, skp, k to end.

Next row K to end, working k1, k1 tbl into yo2.

K 8 rows.

Bind off.

ARMBANDS

Mark a point 8(8¼:8¾)in/20(21:22)cm down from upper arm seam on back and front.

With size 3 (3.25mm) needles, pick up and k 79(83:87) sts between markers.

K 2 rows.

Bind off knitwise on wrong side.

TO FINISH

Sew side and armband seams. Sew on button.

Back & Fronts

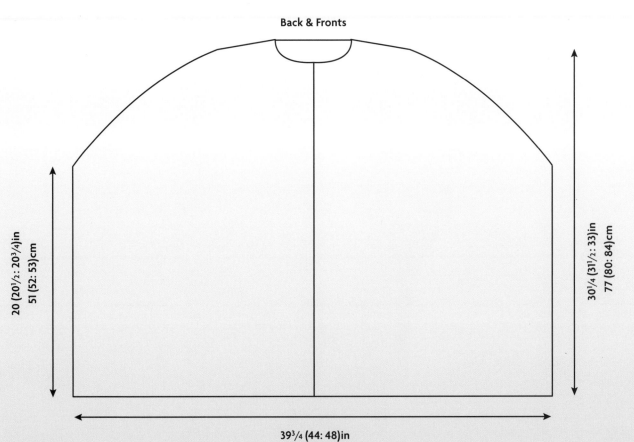

20 (20¹/₂: 20³/₄)in
51 (52: 53)cm

30¹/₄ (31¹/₂: 33)in
77 (80: 84)cm

39³/₄ (44: 48)in
101 (112: 122)cm

Storage Jar Bands

This dainty pattern is wonderful for using up any leftover yarns that you may have lying around the house. These little bands will transform all your storage jars, turning something practical and often cluttered into attractive and sophisticated items. They can be adapted to fit any size jar, and as they are small accessories that require minimum time and effort to complete, you will soon find that they become a necessity throughout all the rooms in your home.

SIZES
To fit jars with a diameter of 4in/10cm and heights of 4in/10cm and 6¼in/16cm (see Notes).

MATERIALS
* One 1¾ oz (50g) ball of Debbie Bliss Rialto 4-Ply in Silver 27
* Pair of size 2 (2.75mm) knitting needles

GAUGE
31.5 sts and 44 rows to 4in/10cm square over patt using size 2 (2.75mm) needles.

ABBREVIATIONS
See page 11.

NOTES

The pattern is worked over a multiple of 9 sts plus an extra
4 sts.
We used small and medium-size glass storage jars. If you are
using different sized jars, you will need to adjust the number of
stitches.

TO MAKE

The band is worked from the top down.
With size 2 (2.75mm) needles, cast on 94 sts.
1st row (wrong side) Purl.
2nd row K3, [yo, k2, skp, k2tog, k2, yo, k1] 10 times, k1.
3rd row Purl.
4th row K2, [yo, k2, skp, k2tog, k2, yo, k1] 10 times, k2.
These 4 rows **form** the patt and are repeated throughout.
Work in patt until piece measures 1½in/4cm for short jar or
3½in/9cm for taller jar, ending with a right-side row.
Bind off knitwise.

TO FINISH

Sew together row-end edges of the knitting to form a tube.
Slip the band over the jar, with the straight bound-off edge at
the base.

Sleep Mask

Nothing quite beats the restorative powers of a deep sleep, but in these hectic times it is often difficult to shut out the outside world. This cashmere and wool blend mask with a velour edging will help to lull you off to sleep, taking you to your own private dreamland. Using less than one ball of yarn, the sleep mask can easily be made in just a few hours, so if you start it in the afternoon you could be counting wooly sheep by bedtime.

SIZE
Approximately 2 ³⁄₄in x 7in/7cm x 18cm.

MATERIALS
* One 1 ³⁄₄ oz (50g) ball of Debbie Bliss Baby Cashmerino in Light Blue 202
* Pair of size 3 (3.25mm) knitting needles
* Piece of cotton fabric for lining, 4in x 8in/10cm x 20cm, and piece of thin batting the same size
* ¹⁄₂yd/50cm of soft elastic, ⁵⁄₈in/15mm wide
* ¹⁄₂yd/50cm of ready-made velvet piping—enclosed 11mm velvet insertion braid 6004
* Sewing needle and thread to match lining fabric

GAUGE
25 sts and 34 rows to 4in/10cm square over patt using size 3 (3.25mm) needles.

ABBREVIATIONS
See page 11.

TO MAKE

With size 3 (3.25mm) needles, cast on 12 sts.

1st and every foll wrong-side row (wrong side) P to end.

2nd row K1, M1, [p1, k3] twice, p1, k1, M1, k1. **14 sts.**

4th row K1, M1, [k3, p1] 3 times, M1, k1. **16 sts.**

6th row K1, M1, k2, [p1, k3] 3 times, M1, k1. **18 sts.**

8th row K1, M1, k1, [p1, k3] 4 times. **19 sts.**

10th row K1, [p1, k3] 4 times, p1, k1.

11th row P to end.

12th row K3, [p1, k3] 4 times.

13th row P to end.

The 10th–13th rows **set** the patt and are repeated once more.
Now, keeping patt correct, dec 1 st at beg of next 8 right-side rows, working the decs as k2tog tbl. **11 sts.**

Patt 7 rows without shaping, so ending with a p row.
Now, keeping patt correct, inc 1 st at beg of next 8 right-side rows, working the incs as k1, M1. **19 sts.**

Patt 9 rows without shaping, so ending with a p row.

Next row (right side) K2tog tbl, k1, [p1, k3] 4 times. **18 sts.**

P1 row.

Next row K2tog tbl, k2, [p1, k3] 3 times, k2tog. **16 sts.**

P1 row.

Next row K2tog tbl, [k3, p1] 3 times, k2tog. **14 sts.**

P1 row.

Next row K2tog tbl, [p1, k3] twice, p1, k1, k2tog. **12 sts.**

Bind off all sts knitwise.

TO FINISH

Using the knitted piece as a template, cut a paper shape. Cut a piece of batting the same size. Then cut a piece of fabric the same size, but adding a ¼in/5mm seam allowance all around. Lay the batting on the fabric, then fold the seam allowance over the batting and baste in place, close to the edge—you will need to clip the seam allowance where necessary. Sew one end of the elastic in place to the wrong side of the padded fabric (mask lining), then allow approximately 14¼in/36cm of elastic free before sewing the other end to the opposite side of the mask. Sew velvet piping to the edge of the mask lining. Lay the knitted piece on the wrong side of the mask lining and easing to fit, sew close to the edge of the piping.

Pouf

This soft and squishy knitted pouf provides the perfect spot for some lounging. Worked in seed stitch, the pouf is made using three strands of cotton yarn held together to create a luxurious, over-sized stitch.

If you are unfamiliar with knitting on such a large scale, then make sure you practice first and do not skip the gauge swatch stage. Also, when joining in new balls of yarn, do not add all three new strands at once but try to stagger them so that the joins are as imperceptible as possible.

SIZE
Approximately 15in/38cm tall x 68in/173cm in circumference.

MATERIALS
* Twenty-one 1 ¾ oz (50g) balls of Debbie Bliss Cotton DK in Duck Egg 09
* Pair of long size 13 (9mm) knitting needles or one size 13 (9mm) circular knitting needle
* One queen-size machine-washable polyester duvet for filling pouf (see pg 38 for suggestions for alternative fillings)

GAUGE
11 sts and 17 rows to 4in/10cm square over seed st using size 13 (9mm) needles and three strands of yarn used together.

ABBREVIATIONS
See page 11.

NOTES

If using a circular needle, work backward and forward in rows; do not work in rounds.

The piece is worked in turning rows throughout.

Do not wrap the stitches when turning, but when slipping the stitch after turning, pull the yarn tight to avoid a hole forming.

The pouf will stretch once it is filled, so the recommended gauge does not reflect the finished size.

TO MAKE

With size 13 (9mm) needles or circular needle and three strands of yarn used together, cast on 67 sts.

Seed st row K1, [p1, k1] to end.

This row **forms** seed st and is repeated.

Seed st one row more.

1st row (right side) Seed st to last 9 sts, turn.

2nd row Sl 1 purlwise pulling yarn tight (see Note), seed st to last 9 sts, turn.

3rd row Sl 1 purlwise, seed st last 3 sts, turn.

4th row Sl 1 purlwise, seed st to last 3 sts, turn.

5th row Sl 1 purlwise, seed st to last 9 sts, turn.

6th row Sl 1 purlwise, seed st to last 9 sts, turn.

7th row Sl 1 purlwise, seed st to last 15 sts, turn.

8th row Sl 1 purlwise, seed st to last 15 sts, turn.

9th row Sl 1 purlwise, seed st to end.

10th row Seed st across all sts. **

These 10 rows **form** the patt and are repeated 21 times more, then work 1st–9th rows again.

Bind off all sts in seed st.

TO FINISH

Close the top and the bottom of the piece as follows: working with two strands of yarn and a blunt-tipped sewing needle, insert the needle through the edge st of every 4th row-end, pulling tightly each time to gather, until there is only a small hole in the middle. Start to sew the cast-on edge to bound-off edge, but only for about 2in/5cm at each end, if you sew any farther you will not be able to insert the duvet. Roll the duvet into a pouf shape and insert it into the knitted piece trying to make as even a shape as possible. Continue to sew the seam until it is complete. You do not need to use a duvet, you could also use old pillows or even old knitwear, just make sure whatever you use is clean.

Heated Neck Pillow

This neck pillow will help you to achieve a restorative time of relaxation every night of the week. Reap comfort from the combination of a weighty pillow, paired with the indulgently soft cashmere blend and mingled with the heady smell of the lavender. Shrug off all the aches and pains that you have accumulated over the long day by draping the pillow over the back of your neck and switching off from the stresses of daily life. Trust me, you will be unable to resist the relaxing qualities of it.

SIZE
Approximately 4 3/4 in x 17 1/4 in/12cm x 44cm.

MATERIALS
* Two 1 3/4 oz (50g) balls of Debbie Bliss Cashmerino Aran in Grey 09
* Pair of size 7 (4.5mm) knitting needles
* Piece of muslin, or other fine cotton fabric, 10 3/4 in x 18 1/2 in/27cm x 47cm
* Sewing thread
* Cleaned and dried cherry stones or rice
* Optional dried lavender or lavender essential oil

GAUGE
22 sts and 32 rows to 4in/10cm square over patt using size 7 (4.5mm) needles.

ABBREVIATIONS
wyif = with yarn in front.
Also see page 11.

COVER

With size 7 (4.5mm) needles, cast on 97 sts.

1st row (wrong side) [K1, p1] 3 times, * [k2, p1] twice, [k1, p1] twice; rep from * to last st, k1.

2nd row [K1, p1] twice, * k2, p1, wyif, sl 3 sts purlwise, p1, k2, p1; rep from * to last 3 sts, k1, p1, k1.

3rd row [K1, p1] 3 times, * k1, p3, [k1, p1] 3 times; rep from * to last st, k1.

4th row [K1, p1] twice, * k2, p1, k1, lift yarn strand with needle tip, k1, then take yarn strand over the stitch, k1, p1, k2, p1; rep from * to last 3 sts, k1, p1, k1.

These 4 rows **form** the pattern and are repeated throughout.

Work in patt until piece measures approximately 10 1/4in/26cm, ending with a 4th row.

Bind off in patt.

Sew the cast-on edge to the bound-off edge.

With the seam lying centrally, sew together the row-end edges at one end, leaving the other end open.

PAD

Fold the fabric in half lengthwise and sew together along the long side and across one short side. Fold the open end over onto the wrong side and press. Turn right side out. Mix the lavender into the cherry stones and fill the pad, but not too full, just over halfway, so allowing for the pad to be gently shaped around the neck. Tuck the raw ends of the fabric inside and stitch across the width to enclose the contents.

TO FINISH

Insert the filled pad into the knitted cover.

TO HEAT

Remove the pad from the knitted cover and heat either in a conventional oven on the lowest possible setting or for a minute or so in a microwave oven on a medium setting. Keep an eye on it and do not overheat.

Cocoon

Armchair Throw

This cozy throw has a wonderfully comforting texture and will brighten any armchair. I have made it in a luxurious purple with a contrasting red trim, but it will work in any combination of colors, so you can pick those that will suit your room. Perfect for curling up with, this throw will require a little time and a fair amount of yarn, but it is an extremely simple pattern and the end result will prove it to be well worth the effort.

SIZE
Approximately 27 1/2in x 54 1/4in/70cm x 138cm.

MATERIALS
* Ten 1 3/4 oz (50g) hanks of Debbie Bliss Paloma in Cyclaman 13 (A) and three hanks in Ruby 15 (B)
* One long size 15 (10mm) circular knitting needle

GAUGE
11 sts and 19 rows to 4in/10cm square over seed st using size 15 (10mm) needles.

ABBREVIATIONS
See page 11.

NOTE
When changing color, twist yarns on wrong side to avoid holes.

TO MAKE

With size 15 (10mm) circular needle and B, cast on 77 sts.

Work backward and forward in rows.

K 11 rows.

Now work in patt as follows:

1st row (right side) K9B, with A, k1, [p1, k1] to last 9 sts, k9B.

This row **forms** the seed st in main color (A) with garter st border in contrasting color (B) and is repeated.

Cont in patt until work measures 52in/132cm from cast-on edge, ending with a wrong-side row.

With B, k 10 rows.

Bind off knitwise.

Trapper Hat

While out and about keep yourself nice and warm by wearing this fashionable trapper hat. Practical yet stylish, it is lined with a layer of fur that will ensure the cold weather does not reach your head and ears. Although this may appear a slightly complicated and almost daunting process, it is actually split into different stages. The ears flaps and peak are knitted first then worked together with the crown.

SIZE
To fit medium-sized adult head.

MATERIALS
* Two 1¾oz (50g) balls of Debbie Bliss Cashmerino Aran in Ruby 610
* Pair of size 8 (5mm) knitting needles
* Piece of black fur fabric for lining, approximately 18in x 33in/51cm x 84cm

GAUGE
18 sts and 24 rows to 4in/10cm square over St st using size 8 (5mm) needles.

ABBREVIATIONS
See page 11.

EARFLAPS (make 2)

With size 8 (5mm) needles, cast on 10 sts.

Beg with a k row, work in St st and inc one st at each end of 2nd row and foll 5 rows. **22 sts.**

Work even in St st for 19 rows without shaping.

Leave sts on a holder.

PEAK

With size 8 (5mm) needles, cast on 26 sts.

Beg with a k row, work in St st and inc one st at each end of 2nd row and foll 6 rows. **40 sts.**

Work even in St st for 11 rows without shaping.

Leave sts on a holder.

CROWN

With size 8 (5mm) needles, cast on 8 sts, then k across 22 sts of left earflap, cast on 5 sts, k across 40 sts of peak, cast on 5 sts, k across 22 sts of right earflap, cast on 8 sts. **110 sts.**

Beg with a p row, work 4 rows in St st.

Next row (wrong side) K to end.

Now work in patt as follows:

1st row K3, [p1, k5] to last 5 sts, p1, k4.

2nd row P3, [k1, p1, k1, p3] to last 5 sts, k1, p1, k1, p2.

3rd row K1, [p1, k3, p1, k1] to last st, p1.

4th row K2, [p5, k1] to end.

5th row Rep 3rd row.

6th row Rep 2nd row.

These 6 rows **form** the patt and are repeated.

Patt 18 rows more.

25th row (right side) K3, [p1, k1, k2tog, k2] to last 5 sts, p1, k1, k2tog, k1. **92 sts**

Next row K to end.

Dec row K1, [k4, k2tog] to last st, k1. **77 sts.**

Next row P to end.

Dec row K1, [k3, k2tog] to last st, k1. **62 sts.**

Next row P to end.

Dec row K1, [k2, k2tog] to last st, k1. **47 sts.**

Next row P to end.

Dec row K1, [k1, k2tog] to last st, k1. **32 sts.**

Next row P to end.

Dec row K1, [k2tog] to last st, k1. **17 sts.**

Dec row P2, [p2tog] to last st, p1. **10 sts.**

Cut yarn, thread end through rem sts, pull to gather, and secure.

TO FINISH

Lay the knitted piece on the fur fabric lining and cut around the edge, adding 3⁄8in/5mm all around. Make darts to shape the top of the fabric to mimic the crown of the hat and trim away the excess. Taking a whole stitch at each side into the seam, sew the back seam of the knitted piece. Make two twisted cords 10 1⁄2in/27cm long, attach one to the edge of each earflap. With right sides together, sew the back seam of the lining taking a 3⁄8in/5mm seam allowance. Then turn lining right side out and insert into the hat. Fold approximately 3⁄8in/5mm of lining onto the wrong side and slipstitch it in place all around the edges of the hat, earflaps, and peak.

Slippers

These sweet little slippers are so impressive they will undoubtably evoke a feeling of longing in all your family and friends! Exceptionally plush and comfortable, there is no comparison to a store-bought pair. The slippers are decorated with a beautiful zigzag design executed in a trio of red, purple, and gold and are finished with a fun detail, a purple tassel. These are delightfully snug slippers that will keep your toes toasty and are well worth putting aside a little time to make.

SIZE
To fit ladies shoe size 7½.

MATERIALS
✳ One 1¾ oz (50g) ball of Debbie Bliss Cashmerino Aran in each of Ruby 610 (A), Blackberry 55 (B), Gold 34 (C), Burnt Orange 48 (D), and Mulberry 42 (E)
✳ Pair of size 8 (5mm) knitting needles
✳ One 12in/30cm square of felt
✳ Pair of ladies size 7½ sheepskin insoles

GAUGE
18 sts and 24 rows to 4in/10cm square over St st using size 8 (5mm) needles.

ABBREVIATIONS
See page 11.

TO MAKE

With size 8 (5mm) needles and A, cast on 103 sts.

K 1 row.

Beg with a k row, work in St st as follows:

1st row (right side) With A, k to end.

2nd row With A, p to end.

3rd row [K5A, 1B] 8 times, k1A, k2tog A, k1A, skp A, k1A, [k1B, k5A] 8 times. **101 sts.**

4th row P2A, [p1B, p1A, p3B, p1A] 7 times, p1B, p1A, p2B, p2tog tbl B, p1A, p2tog B, p2B, p1A, p1B, [p1A, p3B, p1A, p1B] 7 times, p2A. **99 sts.**

5th row K4B, [k1C, k1B, k1C, k3B] 7 times, k1C, k2tog B, k1C, skp B, k1C, [k3B, k1C, k1B, k1C] 7 times, k4B. **97 sts.**

6th row P2C, [p1B, p5C] 7 times, p1B, p1C, p2tog tbl C, p1C, p2tog C, p1C, p1B, [p5C, p1B] 7 times, p2C. **95 sts.**

7th row [K2D, k1C] 15 times, k2tog D, k1D, skp D, [k1C, k2D] 15 times. **93 sts.**

8th row [P5D, p1A] 7 times, p2D, p2tog tbl D, p1D, p2tog D, p2D, [p1A, p5D] 7 times. **91 sts.**

9th row K2D, [k1A, k1D, k3A, k1D] 6 times, k1A, k1D, k3A, k2tog D, k1A, skp D, k3A, k1D, k1A, [k1D, k3A, k1D, k1A] 6 times, k2D. **89 sts.**

10th row P4A, [p1B, p1A, p1B, p3A] 6 times, p1B, p1A, p2tog tbl B, p1A, p2tog B, p1A, p1B, [p3A, p1B, p1A, p1B] 6 times, p4A. **87 sts.**

11th row K3A, [k2B, k1A] 12 times, k2B, k2tog B, k1B, skp B, k2B, [k1A, k2B] 12 times, k3A. **85 sts.**

12th row [P2C, p1B] 13 times, p1C, p2tog tbl C, p1B, p2tog C, p1C, [p1B, p2C] 13 times. **83 sts.**

13th row K4C, [k3E, k3C] 5 times, k3E, k2C, k2tog C, k1C, skp C, k2C, k3E, [k3C, k3E] 5 times, k4C. **81 sts.**

14th row P2E, [p1C, p5E] 6 times, p2tog tbl C, p1C, p2tog C, [p5E, p1C] 6 times, p2E. **79 sts.**

15th row K2D, [k1E, k2D] 11 times, k1E, k1D, k2tog D, k1E, skp D, k1D, k1E, [k2D, k1E] 11 times, k2D. **77 sts.**

16th row P4A, [p3D, p3A] 5 times, p2D, p2tog tbl D, p1A, p2tog D, p2D, [p3A, p3D] 5 times, p4A. **75 sts.**

17th row K5A, [k1D, k5A] 5 times, k2tog D, k1A, skp D, [k5A, k1D] 5 times, k5A. **73 sts.**

18th row P34A, p2tog tbl A, p1A, p2tog A, p34A. **71 sts.**

19th row (right side) P33A, p2tog A, p1A, p2tog tbl A, p33A. **69 sts.**

Bind off knitwise.

TO FINISH

Sew back seam.

Using the sheepskin insoles as a guide, draw around the edge, adding a $3/8$in/3mm seam allowance, to make a paper template. Then cut two pieces of felt using the template. Mark the center of the heel edge. Stitch the cast-on edge of the slipper to the felt, making sure the back seam matches the heel marker. Insert the insole into the slipper. Make a small tassel from yarn and sew to the top of the back seam.

Slouchy Hat

Right on trend, this fashionable hat is extremely simple to make and requires only a few balls of yarn. Worked in an aran-weight yarn, which is made from an extra fine merino wool, this hat has a wonderfully silky texture and is gorgeously soft to the touch. The yarn is ideal for this project as the extra-fine wool creates the desired slouch at the back of the hat as well as having enough stretch to ensure that it will fit comfortably.

SIZE
One size to fit an average-sized adult head.

MATERIALS
* Three 1 ¾ oz (50g) balls of Debbie Bliss Rialto Aran in Royal 38 (A) and one ball in Red 18 (B)
* Pair each of size 6 (4mm) and size 8 (5mm) knitting needles

GAUGE
18 sts and 24 rows to 4in/10cm square over St st using size 8 (5mm) needles.

ABBREVIATIONS
See page 11.

TO MAKE

With size 6 (4mm) needles and B, cast on 102 sts.

1st rib row (right side) P1, [k1, p1, k1, p2] to last st, k1.

2nd rib row P1, [k2, p1, k1, p1] to last st, k1.

These 2 rows **form** the rib and are repeated.

Work 9 rows more in rib, so ending with 1st rib row.

Inc row (wrong side) P1, [k2, p1, k1, M1, p1] to last st, k1. **122 sts.**

Change to size 8 (5mm) needles.

Change to A.

1st row K to end.

2nd row P1, [k2, p1] to last st, k1.

3rd row P1, [k1, p2] to last st, k1.

These last 2 rows **form** the rib and are repeated.

Work 43 rows more in rib as now set, ending with a 2nd rib row.

Dec row P1, [k1, p2, k1, p2tog] to last st, k1. **102 sts.**

Work 3 rows more in rib as set.

Dec row P1, [k1, p2tog, k1, p1] to last st, k1. **82 sts.**

Work 3 rows more in rib as set.

Dec row P1, * sl 1, k2tog, psso, p1, [k1, p1] twice; rep from * to last st, k1. **62 sts.**

Work 3 rows more in rib as set.

Dec row P1, [k1, p1, k1, p3tog] to last st, k1. **42 sts.**

Work 3 rows more in rib as set.

Dec row P1, * sl 1, k2tog, psso, p1; rep from * to last st, k1. **22 sts.**

Next row P1, [p2tog] 10 times, p1. **12 sts.**

Cut yarn, thread through rem sts, pull to gather, and secure, then sew seam.

Chair Back

Give your chair a new lease of life with this ingenius gold cover. It will take a bit of time to make so set yourself aside plenty of me-time, especially if you are wanting to make a set. The thick and chunky style cable knit will last well with long wear and give added comfort. The stylish leather ties that run down both sides add a decorative detail, and will ensure the knit holds a good shape over time.

SIZE
Approximately 17in x 37³⁄₄in/43cm x 96cm.

MATERIALS
✱ Ten 1³⁄₄ oz (50g) balls of Debbie Bliss Rialto Chunky in Gold 07
✱ Pair of size 10¹⁄₂ (6.5mm) knitting needles
✱ Cable needle
✱ 2¹⁄₂yd/2.2m of leather strip (or ribbon)

GAUGE
15 sts and 21 rows to 4in/10cm square over St st using size 10¹⁄₂ (6.5mm) needles.

ABBREVIATIONS
bind 3 = yarn to back of work, sl 1, k1, yo, k1, pass the slipped st over the [k1, yo, k1].
MB = pick up loop lying between st just worked and next st on left-hand needle, k into back, front, and back of loop, turn, p3, turn, k3, turn, p1, p2tog, turn, k2tog.

C4B = slip next 2 sts onto cable needle and hold at back of work, k2, then k2 from cable needle.
C4F = slip next 2 sts onto cable needle and hold to front of work, k2, then k2 from cable needle.
C6B = slip next 3 sts onto cable needle and hold at back of work, k3, then k3 from cable needle.
C6F = slip next 3 sts onto cable needle and hold to front of work, k3, then k3 from cable needle.
C3BP = slip next st onto cable needle and hold at back of work, k2, then p1 from cable needle.
C3FP = slip next 2 sts onto cable needle and hold to front of work, p1, then k2 from cable needle.
C4BP = slip next st onto cable needle and hold at back of work, k3, then p1 from cable needle.
C4FP = slip next 3 sts onto cable needle and hold to front of work, p1, then k3 from cable needle.
C5BP = slip next 2 sts onto cable needle and hold at back of work, k3, then p2 from cable needle.
C5FP = slip next 3 sts onto cable needle and hold to front of work, p2, then k3 from cable needle;
cluster 6 = k next 6 sts and slip them onto a cable needle, wrap yarn 4 times counterclockwise around these 6 sts, slip sts back onto right-hand needle.
Also see page 11.

PANEL A

This panel is worked over 20 sts.

1st row Bind 3, p4, k6, p4, bind 3.

2nd row P3, k4, p6, k4, p3.

3rd row Bind 3, p4, C6B, p4, bind 3.

4th row P3, k4, p6, k4, p3.

5th row Bind 3, p3, C4BP, C4FP, p3, bind 3.

6th row P3, k3, p3, k2, p3, k3, p3.

7th row C5FP, C4BP, p2, C4FP, C5BP.

8th row K2, p6, k4, p6, k2.

9th row P2, C6B, p4, C6F, p2.

10th row Rep 8th row.

11th row [C5BP, C5FP] twice.

12th row Rep 2nd row.

13th row K3, p4, cluster 6, p4, k3.

14th row Rep 2nd row.

15th row [C5FP, C5BP] twice.

16th–18th rows Rep 8th–10th rows.

19th row C5BP, C4FP, p2, C4BP, C5FP.

20th row Rep 6th row.

21st row Bind 3, p3, C4FP, C4BP, p3, bind 3.

22nd–24th rows Rep 2nd–4th rows.

25th–28th rows [Rep 1st and 2nd rows] twice.

These 28 rows **form** the patt and are repeated throughout.

PANEL B

This panel is worked over 40 sts.

1st row P3, MB, p1, pass bobble st over the p1, p2, k4, [p4, MB, p1, pass bobble st over the p1, p3, k4] twice, p3, MB, p1, pass bobble st over the p1, p2.

2nd row K6, p4, [k8, p4] twice, k6.

3rd row P6, C4B, [p8, C4B] twice, p6.

4th row K6, p4, [k8, p4] twice, k6.

5th row P5, C3BP, C3FP, [p6, C3BP, C3FP] twice, p5.

6th row K5, p2, k2, p2, [k6, p2, k2, p2] twice, k5.

7th row P4, [C3BP, p2, C3FP, p4] 3 times.

8th row K4, [p2, k4] 6 times.

9th row P3, C3BP, p4, C3FP, [p2, C3BP, p4, C3FP] twice, p3.

10th row K3, p2, k6, p2, [k2, p2, k6, p2] twice, k3.

11th row P2, [C3BP, p6, C3FP] 3 times, p2.

12th row K2, [p2, k8, p2] 3 times, k2.

13th row P2, k2, p8, [C4B, p8] twice, k2, p2.

14th row Rep 12th row.

15th row P2, k2, p4, MB, p1, pass bobble st over the p1, p3, [k4, p4, MB, p1, pass bobble st over the p1, p3] twice, k2, p2.

16th–18th rows Rep 12th–14th rows.

19th row P2, [C3FP, p6, C3BP] 3 times, p2.

20th row Rep 10th row.

21st row P3, C3FP, p4, C3BP, [p2, C3FP, p4, C3BP] twice, p3.

22nd row Rep 8th row.

23rd row P4, [C3FP, p2, C3BP, p4] 3 times.

24th row Rep 6th row.

25th row P5, C3FP, C3BP, [p6, C3FP, C3BP] twice, p5.

26th row Rep 4th row.

27th row P6, C4B, [p8, C4B] twice, p6.

28th row K6, p4, [k8, p4] twice, k6.

These 28 rows **form** the patt and are repeated throughout.

TO MAKE

With size 10½ (6.5mm) needles, cast on 77 sts.

P 3 rows.

Inc row P5, k4, p1, M1, p2, M1, p1, k4, p3, k6, p2, M1, p1, [k8, p2, M1, p1] twice, k6, p3, k4, p1, M1, p2, M1, p1, k4, p5. **84 sts.**

Now work in patt as follows:

1st row (right side) P2, work across 1st row of Panels A, B, A, p2.

2nd row P2, work across 2nd row of Panels A, B, A, p2.

These 2 rows **set** the panels with garter st edges.

Cont in patt until work measures 37½in/95cm from cast-on edge, ending with a 1st patt row.

Dec row P5, k4, p1, [p2tog] twice, p1, k4, p3, k6, p1, p2tog, p1, [k8, p1, p2tog, p1] twice, k6, p3, k4, p1, [p2tog] twice, p1, k4, p5. **77 sts.**

P 2 rows.

Bind off purlwise.

TO FINISH

Cut the leather strip into eight equal lengths. With the knitted piece placed over the chair, thread four leather strips through the edges of the knitting down each side of the cover as shown and tie to hold in place.

Cowl

The cowl has become a very popular fashion item in the last few years and is a great accessory for cold, wet weather. Staying away from the dreary blacks, browns, and grays that are often present in autumn and winter wardrobes, here I have used a refreshing and somewhat surprising combination of colors—a bright pink mixed with a burnt orange. Knitted in my favorite seed stitch, there is no shaping required for this cowl.

SIZE
Approximately 13¾in/35cm wide x 43¼in/100cm long.

MATERIALS
✳ Three 1¾ oz (50g) hanks of Debbie Bliss Paloma in each of Hot Pink 16 (A) and Burnt Orange 17 (B)
✳ Pair of size 19 (15mm) knitting needles

GAUGE
7.5 sts and 12 rows to 4in/10cm square over seed st using size 19 (15mm) needles and two strands of yarn used together.

ABBREVIATIONS
See page 11.

TO MAKE

With size 19 (15mm) needles and one strand of A and one strand of B used together, cast on 26 sts.

1st row (right side) [K1, p1] to end.

2nd row [P1, k1] to end.

These 2 rows **form** the seed st patt and are repeated.

Cont in patt until piece measures approximately 43¼in/100cm or until you have just enough yarn remaining to work the bind-off row.

Bind off in seed st.

TO FINISH

Sew cast-on edge to bound-off edge.

Cabled Socks

A treat for your feet, these cabled socks are a touch of pure luxury. Not only stylish, with attached pompoms they are great fun, too! Made from supple Baby Cashmerino and knitted in a simple yet effective cabled texture, these socks are perfect for lazing around the house and look cheeky peeking out the top of a pair of boots. In fact, these are so comfy it will be hard to make yourself take these off at the end of the day so you will probably end up wearing them to bed, too!

SIZE
To fit ladies shoe sizes 6½–7½ (7½–8½).

MATERIALS
* 6(7) 1¾ oz (50g) balls of Debbie Bliss Baby Cashmerino in Sienna 67
* Pair of size 3 (3.25mm) knitting needles
* Set of four size 3 (3.25mm) double-pointed knitting needles
* Cable needle

GAUGE
25 sts and 34 rows to 4in/10cm square over St st using size 3 (3.25mm) needles.

ABBREVIATIONS
C11B = slip next 6 sts onto cable needle and hold at back of work, k5, slip the purl st back onto left hand needle, p this st, then k5 from cable needle.
C2BP = slip next st onto cable needle and hold at back of work, k1, then p1 from cable needle.
C2FP = slip next st onto cable needle and hold to front of work, p1, then k1 from cable needle.
Also see page 11.

TO MAKE

With size 3 (3.25mm) needles, cast on 79 sts.

1st row (right side) K2, [p2, C2BP, k1, C2FP, p2, k2] to end.

2nd row P2, [k2, p1, k1, p1, k1, p1, k2, p2] to end.

3rd row K2, [p1, C2BP, p1, k1, p1, C2FP, p1, k2] to end.

4th row P2, [k1, p1, k2, p1, k2, p1, k1, p2] to end.

5th row K2, [C2BP, p2, k1, p2, C2FP, k2] to end.

6th row P2, [p1, k3, p1, k3, p3] to end.

Rep the last 6 rows 3 times more and the first 5 rows again.

Inc row (wrong side) P1, M1, p1, [p1, k1, M1, k1, M1, k1, p1, k1, M1, k1, M1, k1, p2, M1, p1] to end. **115 sts.**

Now work in cable patt as follows:

1st row K3, [p1, k5, p1, k5, p1, k3] to end.

2nd row P3, [k1, p5, k1, p5, k1, p3] to end.

3rd–6th rows [Rep 1st and 2nd rows] twice.

7th row K3, [p1, C11B, p1, k3] to end.

8th row Rep 2nd row.

9th–14th rows Rep 1st and 2nd rows 3 times.

These 14 rows **form** the patt and are repeated.

Work even in patt until sock measures 14in/35cm, ending with a 6th row.

Dec row K1, k2tog, * p1, slip next 6 sts onto cable needle and hold at back of work, [k next st from left-hand needle tog with 1 st on cable needle] 5 times, slip "p" st back onto left-hand needle, p this st tog with next st on left hand needle, k2tog, k1; rep from * to end. **65 sts.**

Next row P2, [k1, p5, k1, p2] to end.

Next row K2, [p1, k5, p1, k2] to end.

Rep the last 2 rows once more.

Next row P2, [k1, p1, p2tog, p2, k1, p2] to end. **58 sts.**

Next row K2, [p1, k4, p1, k2] to end.

Next row P2tog, [k1, p4, k1, p2] to last 7 sts, k1, p3, k1, p2tog. **56 sts.**

Cut yarn.

Divide sts onto 3 double-pointed needles as follows: slip first 14 sts onto first needle, next 14 sts onto second needle, and next 14 sts onto 3rd needle, slip last 14 sts onto other end of first needle.

Heel flap

With right side facing, join yarn to 28 sts on first needle. Work on these 28 sts only.

Beg with a k row, work 15 rows in St st.

Shape heel

** Next row Sl 1, p to end.

Next row Sl 1, k16, skp, k1, turn.

Next row Sl 1, p7, p2tog, p1, turn.

Next row Sl 1, k8, skp, k1, turn.

Next row Sl 1, p9, p2tog, p1, turn.

Next row Sl 1, k10, skp, k1, turn.

Next row Sl 1, p11, p2tog, p1, turn.

Next row Sl 1, k12, skp, k1, turn.

Next row Sl 1, p13, p2tog, p1, turn.

Next row Sl 1, k14, skp, k1, turn.

Next row Sl 1, p15, p2tog, p1, turn. **18 sts.**

Foot shaping

With right side facing, k18, pick up and k 12 sts along side of heel flap, place a marker, k28 from 2nd and 3rd needles, place a marker, pick up and k 12 sts along other side of heel flap. **70 sts.** Arrange these sts evenly on 3 needles and cont in rounds as follows:

Round 1 K to within 2 sts of marker, k2tog, slip marker, k to next marker, slip marker, skp, k to end.

Round 2 K to end.

Rep the last 2 rounds 6 times more. **56 sts.**

Slipping markers on every round, work even until sock measures 7(7 1/2)in/18(19)cm from back of heel.

Shape toe

Round 1 K to within 3 sts of marker k2tog, k1, slip marker, k1, skp, k to within 3 sts of next marker, k2tog, k1, slip marker, k1, skp, k to end.

Round 2 K to end.

Rep the last 2 rounds until 32 sts rem.

Slip first 8 sts onto one needle, next 16 sts onto a second needle, then rem 8 sts onto end of first needle.

Transfer the two groups of sts onto safety pins, fold sock inside out, then transfer the sts back onto two needles and bind off one st from each needle together. Sew cuff leg and ankle seam. Make two twisted cords approximately 25in/64cm long. Make four pompoms. Weave each cord in and out around the sock just below the cuff and attach the pompoms to each end.

Waterfall Jacket

The tumbling, rippling lapels of this soft unstructured jacket echo the undulations of water, hence its name. Made in a blended yarn of baby alpaca and silk, the jacket is so warming and cozy that you simply will not ever want to take it off. Worked in stockinette stitch, with seed stitch borders for just a hint of texture, this garment only needs minimal shaping so is a breeze to make. And the roomy patch pockets are the perfect hiding place for indulgent treats.

SIZE

To fit bust

32	34	36	38	40	42	44	46	in
81	86	92	97	102	107	112	117	cm

Finished measurements

Width across back

20	21¼	22½	23	24½	25½	26¾	27½	in
51	54	57½	59½	62	65	67½	70	cm

Length to shoulder

29½	30	30¼	30¼	31	31¼	32	32¼	in
75	76	77	78	79	80	81	82	cm

Sleeve length 17in/43cm for all sizes

MATERIALS

* 21(22:23:24:25:26:27:28) 1¾ oz (50g) hanks of Debbie Bliss Andes in Maroon 20
* Pair each of size 3 (3.25mm) and size 6 (4mm) knitting needles
* One size 3 (3.25mm) circular knitting needle

GAUGE

22 sts and 30 rows to 4in/10cm square over St st using size 6 (4mm) needles.

ABBREVIATIONS

See page 11.

BACK

With size 3 (3.25mm) needles, cast on
115(121:127:133:139:145:151:157) sts.
Seed st row (right side) K1, [p1, k1] to end.
Rep this row for 2¼in/6cm, ending with a wrong-side row.
Change to size 6 (4mm) needles.
Beg with a k row, work in St st until back measures 22in/56cm
from cast-on edge, ending with a p row.
Shape armholes
Bind off 6(6:7:7:8:8:9:9) sts at beg of next 2 rows.
103(109:113:119:123:129:133:139) sts.
Next row K2, skp, k to last 4 sts, k2tog, k2.
Next row P to end.
Rep the last 2 rows 4(5:5:6:6:7:7:8) times.
93(97:101:105:109:113:117:121) sts.
Work even until back measures
28¾(29¼:29½:30:30¼:30¾:31:31½)in/
73(74:75:76:77:78:79:80)cm from cast-on edge, ending with
a p row.
Shape upper arms and shoulders
Bind off 4 sts at beg of next 8 rows. **61(65:69:73:77:81:85:89) sts.**
Bind off 6(6:7:7:8:8:9:9) sts at beg of next 2 rows and
6(7:7:8:8:9:9:10) sts at beg of foll 2 rows.
Leave rem 37(39:41:43:45:47:49:51) sts on a holder.

POCKET LININGS (make 2)

With size 6 (4mm) needles, cast on 31(31:31:31:33:33:33:33) sts.
Beg with a k row, work 30 rows in St st.
Leave these sts on a spare needle.

LEFT FRONT

With size 3 (3.25mm) needles, cast on
121(125:129:133:137:141:145:149) sts.
Seed st row (right side) K1, [p1, k1] to end.
Rep this row for 2¼in/6cm, ending with a wrong-side row.
Change to size 6 (4mm) needles.
1st row K to last 9 sts, seed st 9.
2nd row Seed st 9, p to end.
These 2 rows **form** the St st with seed st border and are
repeated.

Work 82 rows more as set.
Place pocket
Next row K31(33:35:37:38:40:42:44), slip next 31(31:31:31:33:33:33:33)
sts onto a holder, k across 31(31:31:31:33:33:33:33) sts of first
pocket lining, k50(52:54:56:57:59:61:63), seed st 9.
Work even until front measures 22in/56cm from cast-on edge,
ending with a wrong-side row.
Shape armhole
Next row Bind off 6(6:7:7:8:8:9:9) sts, k to last 9 sts, seed st 9.
115(119:122:126:129:133:136:140) sts.
Next row Seed st 9, p to end.
Next row K2, skp, k to last 9 sts, seed st 9.
Rep the last 2 rows 4(5:5:6:6:7:7:8) times.
110(113:116:119:122:125:128:131) sts.
Work even until front measures same as Back to upper arm and
shoulder shaping, ending at armhole edge.
Shape upper arm and shoulder
Bind off 4 sts at beg of next row and 3 foll right-side rows.
94(97:100:103:106:109:112:115) sts.
Work 1 row.
Bind off 6(6:7:7:8:8:9:9) sts at beg of next row and 6(7:7:8:8:9:9:10)
sts at beg of foll right-side row.
Work 1 row.
Leave rem 82(84:86:88:90:92:94:96) sts on a holder.

RIGHT FRONT

With size 3 (3.25mm) needles, cast on
121(125:129:133:137:141:145:149) sts.
Seed st row (right side) K1, [p1, k1] to end.
Rep this row for 2¼in/6cm, ending with a wrong-side row.
Change to size 6 (4mm) needles.
1st row Seed st 9, k to end.
2nd row P to last 9 sts, seed st 9.
These 2 rows **form** the St st with seed st border and are
repeated.

Work 82 rows more as set.

Place pocket

Next row Seed st 9, k50(52:54:56:57:59:61:63), slip
next 31(31:31:31:33:33:33:33) sts onto a holder, k across
31(31:31:31:33:33:33:33) sts of second pocket lining,
k31(33:35:37:38:40:42:44).

Work even until front measures 22in/56cm from cast-on edge,
ending with a right-side row.

Shape armhole

Next row Bind off 6(6:7:7:8:8:9:9) sts, patt to end.
115(119:122:126:129:133:136:140) sts.

Next row Seed st 9, k to last 4 sts, k2tog, k2.

Next row P to last 9 sts, seed st 9.

Rep the last 2 rows 4(5:5:6:6:7:7:8) times.
110(113:116:119:122:125:128:131) sts.

Work even until front measures same as Back to upper arm and
shoulder shaping, ending at armhole edge.

Shape upper arm and shoulder

Bind off 4 sts at beg of next row and 3 foll wrong-side rows.
94(97:100:103:106:109:112:115) sts.

Work 1 row.

Bind off 6(6:7:7:8:8:9:9) sts at beg of next row and 6(7:7:8:8:9:9:10)
sts at beg of foll wrong-side row.

Work 1 row.

Leave rem 82(84:86:88:90:92:94:96) sts on a holder.

SLEEVES

With size 3 (3.25mm) needles, cast on 41(43:45:47:51:53:55) sts.

Seed st row (right side) K1, [p1, k1] to end.

Rep this row for 2¼in/6cm, ending with a wrong-side row.

Change to size 6 (4mm) needles.

Beg with a k row, work in St st.

Work 2 rows.

Inc row K3, M1, k to last 3 sts, M1, k3.

Work 5 rows.

Rep the last 6 rows 15 times more and the inc row again.
75(77:79:81:83:85:87:89) sts.

Work even until sleeve measures 17in/43cm from cast-on edge,
ending with a p row.

Shape sleeve cap

Bind off 6(6:7:7:8:8:9:9) sts at beg of next 2 rows.

63(65:65:67:67:69:69:71) sts.

Work 2 rows.

Next row K2, skp, k to last 4 sts, k2tog, k2.

Work 3 rows.

Rep the last 4 rows once more.

Next row K2, skp, k to last 4 sts, k2tog, k2.

Next row P to end.

Rep the last 2 rows 4(5:5:6:6:7:7:8) times. **49 sts.**

Bind off 3 sts at beg of next 12 rows.

Bind off rem 13 sts.

NECK EDGING

Sew upper arm and shoulder seams.

With right side facing and size 3 (3.25mm) circular needle, slip
82(84:86:88:90:92:94:96) sts from right front holder onto a
needle, k 37(39:41:43:45:47:49:51) sts from back neck holder, then
patt 82(84:86:88:90:92:94:96) sts from left front holder.
201(207:213:219:225:231:237:243) sts.

Work 7 rows in seed st as set by front borders.

Bind off in seed st.

POCKET TOPS

With right side facing, slip 31(31:31:31:33:33:33:33) sts at top of
pocket onto a size 3 (3.25mm) needle and work 7 rows in
seed st.

Bind off in seed st.

TO FINISH

Sew side and sleeve seams. Sew sleeves into armholes, easing to
fit. Sew down pocket linings and pocket tops.

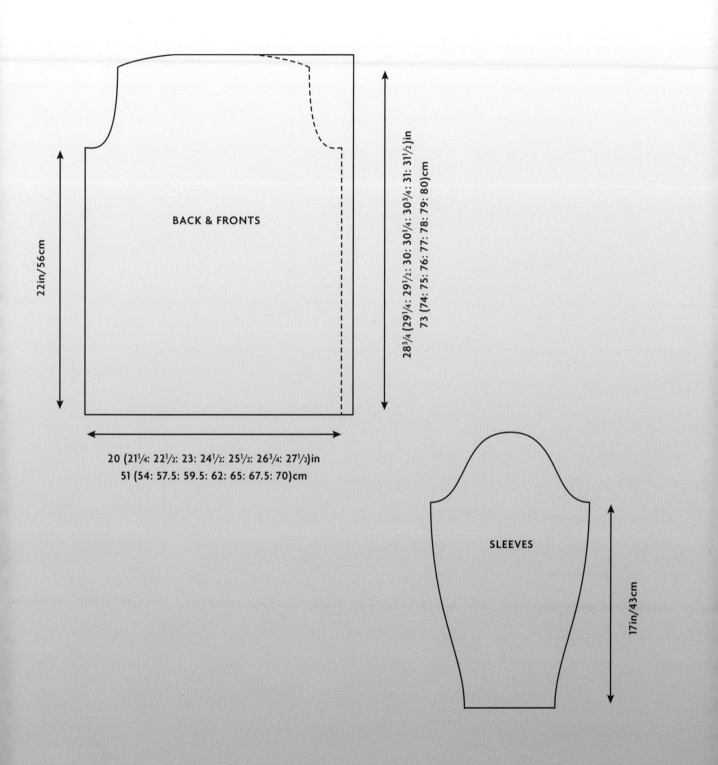

BACK & FRONTS

22in/56cm

28³⁄₄ (29¹⁄₄: 29¹⁄₂: 30: 30¹⁄₄: 30³⁄₄: 31: 31¹⁄₂)in
73 (74: 75: 76: 77: 78: 79: 80)cm

20 (21¹⁄₄: 22¹⁄₂: 23: 24¹⁄₂: 25¹⁄₂: 26³⁄₄: 27¹⁄₂)in
51 (54: 57.5: 59.5: 62: 65: 67.5: 70)cm

SLEEVES

17in/43cm

Detox

Accessories Holder

"A place for everything and everything in its place," this is an adage that, when lived by, can create a happy and harmonious home. This practical tie-up roll provides a stylish storage solution for knitters who need to keep tabs on their equipment. With pockets and divided sections for slotting pairs of knitting needles into—as well as stitch counters and other accessories, including a sewn needlecase—this is a perfectly portable holder that no knitter will want to be without.

SIZE
Approximately 12in x 15¼in/30cm x 39cm.

MATERIALS
* Four 1¾ oz (50g) balls of Debbie Bliss Cotton DK in Avocado 20
* Pair of size 7 (4.5mm) knitting needles
* 1yd/1m of cotton tape or ribbon, ⅝in/15mm wide
* ½yd/50cm of fabric for lining (see Note)
* Piece of felt, 7in x 8¾in/18cm x 22cm, for needle case (optional)
* Sewing thread and needle

GAUGE
24 sts and 26 rows to 4in/10cm square over patt using size 7 (4.5mm) needles.

ABBREVIATIONS
See page 11.

NOTE
For the lining, we used Liberty Classic Tana Lawn in Claire-Aude T (www.liberty.co.uk).

TO MAKE

With size 7 (4.5mm) needles, cast on 74 sts.

1st row (right side) K to end.

2nd row P1, [p2tog but do not slip st off needle, then p the first st again and slip both sts off needle together] to last st, p1.

3rd row K to end.

4th row P2, [p2tog but do not slip st off needle, then p the first st again and slip both sts off needle together] to last 2 sts, p2.

These 4 rows **form** the patt and are repeated throughout.

Work in patt until piece measures 22in/56cm, ending with a 3rd patt row.

Shape for pockets

Next row (wrong side) Bind off 26 sts knitwise, with 1 st on needle after bind-off, p1, [p2tog but do not slip st off needle, then p the first st again and slip both sts off needle together] to last 2 sts, p2. **48 sts.**

Beg with a 1st row, cont in patt for 3 1/4in/8cm more, ending with a right-side row.

Bind off all sts knitwise.

TO FINISH

Using the knitted piece as a template, and making sure you place the wrong side of the lining fabric and wrong side of the knitting together, cut the lining fabric to shape, allowing a 5/8in/1.5cm seam allowance all around. Cut a 2in/5cm piece from the tape (or ribbon) and reserve for the needle case (if making). Fold the remainder of the tape in two, approximately 12in/30cm from one end. Press the seam allowance of the lining onto the wrong side, then folding the corners, hand sew the fabric to the wrong side of the knitted piece, catching the fold of the tape into the seam, approximately 10 3/4in/27cm down from cast-on edge on the left-hand side of the piece. Fold approximately 2 3/4in/7cm of top (unshaped) edge over onto the fabric and slipstitch the sides in place from the fold down to the cast-on edge. Fold the lower edge up onto the fabric, so that the final length of the completed holder is 15 1/4in/39cm, and slipstitch the side edges in place. With sewing thread, stitch individual pockets in the lower section, these can be any width to suit your accessories.

NEEDLE CASE (optional)

Cut a piece of lining fabric and two pieces of felt, approximately 3 1/2in x 4 1/4in/9cm x 11cm. Fold under a 1/2in/1cm seam allowance all around the fabric and press in place, mitering the corners. Fold the fabric in half and mark the center line. Lay the hemmed fabric onto one piece of felt placing it centrally and topstitch around the edges, catching the short piece of tape into the seam to the left of the center line. Lay the other piece of felt centrally on the first (inside of cover) and stitch through all layers along the center line. Using pinking shears, trim the felt of the cover around the edge, then trim the inside piece of felt, slightly smaller, so that when closed, the inner felt does not show around the edge. Stitch the free end of the tape (or ribbon) under the edge of the top flap of the holder.

Message Board

Whether used to hold messages for the rest of the household, notices of things to-do, useful clippings, photos of unforgettable moments, or a combination of all these things, this clever message board will become an invaluable part of your life. Made using only one ball of yarn, this can easily be created in just a single afternoon. Pretty, simple, and useful, this board can be adjusted in size and made in a variety of colors.

SIZE
24in x 16in/60cm x 40cm

MATERIALS
* One 1¾ oz (50g) ball of Debbie Bliss Cotton DK in Mink 52
* Pair of size 5 (3.75mm) knitting needles
* Piece of fabric, approximately 28in x 20in/70cm x 50cm
* Piece of felt or batting, 24in x 16in/60cm x 40cm
* 24in x 16in/60cm x 40cm cork board
* Staple gun and/or strong parcel tape
* Bronzed upholstery nails

ABBREVIATIONS
See page 11.

NOTES
The gauge is not relevant.
Figures in brackets refer to the long lengths, figures before the brackets refer to the shorter lengths.
If you use a different size board, you will need to adjust the length of the strips, fabrics, and the amount of yarn. Our strips used a complete ball of yarn.

TO MAKE

Make 4 short lengths and 4 long lengths.

Leaving a 59(118)in/1.5(3)m length of yarn and using the thumb cast-on method throughout, work as follows:

Cast-on row With size 5 (3.75mm) needles, place a slip knot on the right needle, [cast on 2 sts, lift the first st over the 2nd st and off needle, yo, lift st over yo, cast on one st] 38(76) times. 77(153) sts.

Bind off all sts knitwise.

TO FINISH

Cut the batting or felt to fit within the frame of the board and lay in place. Lay the fabric over the board, folding the excess over onto the back and neatly folding the corners. Then tape or staple the fabric in place to the back of the frame. Measure and mark (with pins) the positions for the knitted strips, then taking the excess over onto the back and pulling to tighten, staple the strips in place—four diagonally in one direction, then the remaining four diagonally in the other, weaving under and over. Apply the upholstery nails where the strips cross. If you prefer, you could also cover the back of the board with felt to neaten.

Double Seed Stitch Tunic

This tunic is created using one of my favorite stitch patterns, double seed stitch. It produces a subtle texture that creates interest in this so very simple top. Worked straight to form subtle capped sleeves and a slit neck, the ribbed hem brings it gently inwards at the bottom. This has a wonderful, integrated garter stitch edge at the neck and sleeve edge.

MEASUREMENTS

To fit bust

32–34	36–38	40–42	44–46	in
81–86	92–97	102–107	112–117	cm

Finished measurements

Bust

38½	41¾	46½	49½	in
98	106	118	126	cm

Length to shoulder

30	30¾	31½	32¼	in
76	78	80	82	cm

MATERIALS

* 14(15:16:17) 1¾ oz (50g) balls of Debbie Bliss Cotton DK in Mint 60
* Pair of each size 5 (3.75mm) and size 6 (4mm) knitting needles
* Pair of size 5 (3.75mm) circular needle, 24in/60cm long

GAUGE

20 sts and 30 rows to 4in/10cm square over double seed st using size 6 (4mm) needles.

ABBREVIATIONS

See page 11.

BACK

With size 5 (3.75mm) needles, cast on 98(106:118:126) sts.

1st row (right side) K2, [p2, k2] to end.

2nd row P2, [k2, p2] to end.

These 2 rows **form** the rib and are repeated.

Work 14 rows more in rib.

Change to size 6 (4mm) needles.

1st row (right side) K2, [p2, k2] to end.

2nd row P2, [k2, p2] to end.

3rd row P2, [k2, p2] to end.

4th row K2, [p2, k2] to end.

These 4 rows **form** the double seed st patt and are repeated.

Cont in patt until back measures 20(20½:21:21¼)in/ 51(52:53:54)cm from cast-on edge, ending with a wrong-side row. **

Now work in patt with garter st edgings as follows:

Next row K2, patt to last 2 sts, k2.

Rep the last row until back measures 30(30¾:31½:32¼)in/ 76(78:80:82)cm from cast-on edge, ending with a wrong-side row.

Shape shoulders

Bind off 6(6:7:7) sts at beg of next 8 rows and 10(13:13:16) sts at beg of foll 2 rows.

Leave rem 30(32:36:38) sts on a spare needle.

FRONT

Work as given for Back to **.

Divide for front opening

Now work in patt with garter st edgings as follows:

Next row (right side) K2, patt 46(50:56:60), k1, turn and work on these sts only for first side of front opening, leave rem sts on a spare needle.

Next row K1, patt to last 2 sts, k2.

Next row K2, patt to last st, k1.

The last 2 rows **form** the patt with garter st edging at front opening and armhole edge and are repeated.

Cont in patt until front measures 26¾(27½:28:28¾)in/ 68(70:71:73)cm from cast-on edge, ending with a wrong-side row.

Shape neck

Next row Patt to last 11 sts, place these 11 sts on a holder, turn and work on rem 38(42:48:52) sts for first side of front neck.

Patt 1 row.

Dec one st at neck edge on every right-side row until 34(37:41:44) sts rem.

Work even until front measures the same as Back to shoulder, ending at armhole edge.

Shape shoulder

Bind off 6(6:7:7) sts at beg of next row and 3 foll right-side rows.

Work 1 row.

Bind off rem 10(13:13:16) sts.

With right side facing, rejoin yarn to rem sts.

Next row (right side) K1, patt to last 2 sts, k2.

Next row K2, patt to last st, k1.

These 2 rows **form** the patt with garter st edging at front opening and armhole edge.

Cont in patt until front measures 26¾(27½:28:28¾)in/ 68(70:71:73)cm from cast-on edge, ending with a wrong-side row.

Shape neck

Next row Patt 11 sts, leave these sts on a holder, patt to end. **38(42:48:52) sts.**

Patt 1 row.

Dec one st at neck edge on every right-side row until 34(37:41:44) sts rem.

Work even until front measures the same as Back to shoulder, ending at armhole edge.

Shape shoulder

Bind off 6(6:7:7) sts at beg of next row and 3 foll wrong-side rows.

Work 1 row.

Bind off rem 10(13:13:16) sts.

NECK EDGING

Sew shoulder seams.

With right side facing and size 5 (3.75mm) circular needle, place 11 sts from right front holder onto needle, pick up and k 23(23:25:25) sts up right front neck, k 30(32:36:38) sts from back neck holder, pick up and k 23(23:25:25) sts down left front neck, patt 11 sts from right front holder. **98(100:108:110) sts.**

K 2 rows.

Bind off knitwise.

TO FINISH

Sew side seams to beginning of armhole edging.

BACK & FRONT

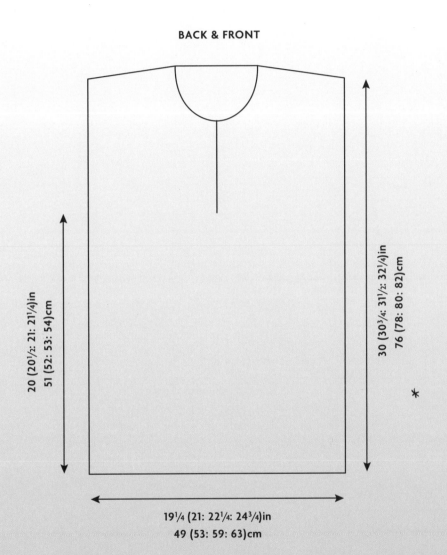

20 (20½: 21: 21¼)in
51 (52: 53: 54)cm

30 (30¾: 31½: 32¼)in
76 (78: 80: 82)cm

*

19¼ (21: 22¼: 24¾)in
49 (53: 59: 63)cm

Storage File

Knitted in a robust cotton yarn, this filing system will transform your storage options. I love the colorful organization that this storage file brings to my work shelves at home, but you do not need to only keep your work and documents in it, you could also use it to store your knitting patterns. Here a lively aqua yarn that is accented with a pretty lining has been used, ensuring that sorting and storing becomes anything but a chore.

SIZE
Approximately 8¾in/22cm wide x 10in/25cm tall.

GAUGE
20½ sts and 28 rows to 4in/10cm over patt using size 6 (4mm) needles.

MATERIALS
* Three 1¾ oz (50g) balls of Debbie Bliss Cotton DK in Aqua 61
* Pair of size 6 (4mm) knitting needles
* Cardboard

ABBREVIATIONS
See page 11.

TO MAKE

With size 6 (4mm) needles, cast on 45 sts and k 1 row.

Now work in patt as follows:

1st row (right side) K1, [p1, k1] to end.

2nd row P1, [k1, p1] to end.

3rd row P1, [k1, p1] to end.

4th row K1, [p1, k1] to end.

These 4 rows **form** the double seed st patt and are repeated.

Cont in patt until piece measures 4in/10cm from cast-on edge, ending with a right-side row.

Foldline row K to end.

Beg with a 1st row, work 4in/10cm in patt, ending with a right-side row.

Foldline row (wrong side) Cast on 22 sts, k to end. **67 sts.**

Next row Cast on 22 sts, k1, [p1, k1] to end. **89 sts.**

Beg with a 2nd row, work in patt for 4in/10cm, ending with a 4th row.

Next row P2tog, patt to last 2 sts, p2tog.

Next row Patt to end.

Rep the last 2 rows until 45 sts rem, ending with a right-side row.

Bind off knitwise.

DIVIDER

With size 6 (4mm) needles, cast on 43 sts.

Beg with a 1st row, work in patt until piece measures approximately 5in/13cm, ending with a right-side row.

Bind off knitwise.

TO FINISH

Following the template, sew edges B to B and D to D first, then sew A to A and C to C.

Using the template, cut the cardboard to shape; try to cut it out in one piece, but if that is not possible, cut the upper part (back and sides) in one piece, then cut out the lower part (base and front). Score the shape along the dotted lines and fold to form the file. Use parcel tape to fix the base and front to the back and sides. To form the divider, cut a piece of cardboard slightly smaller than the width of the inside of the file and to fit the length of the knitted divider piece. Using the template, cut the fabric to shape, adding 5/8in/1.5cm around all the edges. Clip into the corner where side B meets base B and side D meets base D. Sew edges B to B and D to D first, then sew A to A and C to C. Press all seams, then insert lining into the constructed cardboard, folding the excess fabric over onto the outside of the box. Put the lined cardboard shape into the knitted piece and slipstitch the lining to the knitting around the edges. Cover the divider in the same way, slip into the box, and stitch the top corners to the sides of the box.

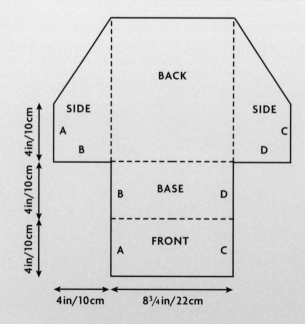

Wine Bottle Covers

Rather than consign your glass bottles to the recycling, give them a new lease of life as covered vases with these witty knitted covers. Choose from the striped, cabled, or Fair Isle styles—or mix and match to create a striking display. With a narrow neck, a bottle takes the agony out of flower arranging as no complicated structure or support is necessary. The beauty of the covers is that they take only a small amount of yarn in various colors, so can be made from the leftovers in your yarn stash.

SIZE
One size to fit a standard 750ml red wine bottle.

MATERIALS
Striped Cover
* One 1 ¾ oz (50g) ball Debbie Bliss Rialto 4-Ply in each of Silver 27 (A), Teal 18 (B), Ecru 02 (C), Dark Red 09 (D), Apple 32 (E), and Navy 13 (F)

Fair Isle Cover
* One 1 ¾ oz (50g) ball Debbie Bliss Rialto 4-Ply in each of Silver 27 (A), Teal 18 (B), Ecru 02 (C), Dark Red 09 (D), Apple 32 (E), and Navy 13 (F)

Cable and Rib Cover
* One 1 ¾ oz (50g) ball Debbie Bliss Rialto 4-Ply in Ecru 02 (C)
* Cable needle
* 3 small buttons

All covers
* Pair each of size 2 (3mm) and size 3 (3.25mm) knitting needles

GAUGE
25 sts and 34 rows over St st, 29 sts and 34 rows over Fair Isle patt, and 33 sts and 45 rows over cable patt, all to 4in/10cm square using size 3 (3.25mm) needles.

YARN NOTE
If you are making all three covers, you will need a total of two balls in Ecru 02 (C) and one ball in each of the remaining five colors.

ABBREVIATIONS
See pages 11 and 104.

STRIPED COVER

With size 2 (3mm) needles and F, cast on 68 sts.

K 1 row.

Change to size 3 (3.25mm) needles.

Beg with a k row, work in St st and stripes of 2 rows A, 2 rows D, 2 rows B, 2 rows C, 2 rows E, and 2 rows F.

Work even until 76 rows have been worked.

Shape top

1st dec row (wrong side) P2, [p2tog, p6] 8 times, p2. **60 sts.**

K 1 row.

2nd dec row P2, [p2tog, p5] 8 times, p2. **52 sts.**

K 1 row.

3rd dec row P2, [p2tog, p4] 8 times, p2. **44 sts.**

K 1 row.

4th dec row P2, [p2tog, p3] 8 times, p2. **36 sts.**

K 1 row.

5th dec row P2, [p2tog, p2] 8 times, p2. **28 sts.**

Neck

Cont in stripe sequence and work 25 rows more.

Bind off knitwise.

Sew seam.

FAIR ISLE COVER

With size 2 (3mm) needles and D, cast on 74 sts.

K 1 row.

Change to size 3 (3.25mm) needles.

Beg with a k row, work in St st and patt from chart until all 40 rows have been worked, then work chart rows 1–21 again, so ending with a right-side row.

Shape top

1st row (wrong side) With A, p2, [p2tog, p6] 9 times. **65 sts.**

2nd row K2A, [1F, 6A] 9 times.

3rd row P5A, [3F, 4A] 8 times, 3 F, 1A.

4th row K2A, [1F, 6A] 9 times.

5th row With A, p2, [p2tog, p5] 9 times. **56 sts.**

6th row With A, k to end.

7th row P1A, [p2tog A, p1A, p1D, p1A, p1D] 9 times, 1A. **47 sts.**

8th row With A, k to end.

9th row With A, p1, [p2tog, p3] 9 times, p1. **38 sts.**

10th row [K1B, K1A] to end.

11th row With A, p to end.

Collar

Cont in A only.

1st row K2, [p2, k2] to end.

2nd row P2, [k2, 2] to end.

Rep the last 2 rows for 8¼in/21cm.

Bind off in rib.

Sew seam, reversing last 4¼in/11cm of seam on collar.

Turn half of collar over.

CHART NOTE

Read chart from right to left on right-side rows and left to right on wrong-side rows. When working in pattern, strand yarn not in use loosely across wrong side of work to keep fabric elastic.

8 STITCH REPEAT

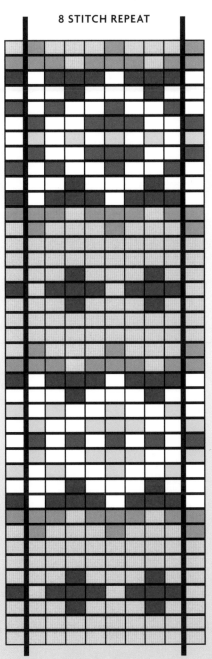

ABBREVIATIONS

C4B = slip next 2 sts onto cable needle and hold at back of work, k2, then k2 from cable needle.

C4F = slip next 2 sts onto cable needle and hold to front of work, k2, then k2 from cable needle.

Also see page 11.

CABLE COVER

With size 2 (3mm) needles and C, cast on 74 sts.

K 1 row.

Change to size 3 (3.25mm) needles and patt.

1st row K2, [p2, k6, p2, k2] to end.

2nd row P to end.

3rd row K2, [p2, C4B, k2, p2, k2] to end.

4th row P to end.

5th row K2, [p2, k2, C4F, p2, k2] to end.

6th row P to end.

The 3rd–6th rows **form** the patt and are repeated.

Work 84 rows more in patt, so ending with a 6th row.

Shape top

1st row K2, [p2tog, C4B, k2, p2tog, k2] to end. **62 sts.**

2nd row P to end.

3rd row K2, [p1, k2, slip next 2 sts onto a cable needle and hold to front of work, k2, then skp from cable needle, p1, k2] to end. **56 sts.**

4th row P to end.

5th row K2, [p1, slip next 2 sts onto a cable needle and hold at back, k2tog, then k2 from cable needle, k1, p1, k2] to end. **50 sts.**

6th row P to end.

7th row K2, [p1, k1, slip next 2 sts onto a cable needle and hold

at front, k1, then skp from cable needle, p1, k2] to end. **44 sts.**

8th row P to end.

9th row K2, [p2tog, k1, p2tog, k2] to end. **32 sts.**

10th row P to end.

11th row K2, [p2tog, p1, k2] to end. **26 sts.**

12th row Cast on 3 sts for button band, p to end. **29 sts.**

Neck

1st row P4, [k2, p2] 5 times, k2, p3.

2nd row P to end.

3rd (buttonhole) row P1, p2tog, yo, p1, [k2, p2] to last 5 sts, k2, p3.

4th row P to end.

5th–18th rows [Rep 1st and 2nd rows] 7 times.

19th (buttonhole) row P1, p2tog, yo, p1, [k2, p2] to last 5 sts, k2, p3.

20th row P to end.

21st–34th rows [Rep 1st and 2nd rows] 7 times.

35th (buttonhole) row P1, p2tog, yo, p1, [k2, p2] to last 5 sts, k2, p3.

36th row P to end.

37th row P4, [k2, p2] 5 times, k2, p3.

38th row P to end.

Bind off in patt.

Sew side seam to beg of neck, then sew cast-on edge of button band behind bottom of buttonhole band. Sew on buttons.

Magazine Holder

Tired of forever having to clear up your widely scattered magazines and bored by tediously hunting for where the magazine with the really great pattern is? Then this sturdy magazine holder provides the perfect solution. Stylish, yet practical, this contemporary holder can store any manner of publications—whether for all your knitting, food, or fashion magazines or even your newspapers. You may even find yourself making one in a different color for each subject.

SIZE
Approximately 26in x 12½in/66cm x 32cm.

MATERIALS
* Four 1¾ oz (50g) balls of Debbie Bliss Cotton DK in Sea Green 59
* Pair of size 6 (4mm) knitting needles
* Piece of heavyweight, stiff buckram, 26in x 12½in/66cm x 32cm
* Piece of fabric for lining, 27¼in x 13¾in/69cm x 35cm
* Sewing thread
* Four 11in/28cm lengths of ribbon, ½in/1cm wide

GAUGE
20 sts and 35 rows to 4in/10cm square over main patt garter st using size 6 (4mm) needles.

ABBREVIATIONS
See page 11.

NOTE
Join on a new ball of yarn between the border and center panel, not at the edge. The knitted piece will be slightly shorter than the buckram stiffening, to ensure a fit tight.

TO MAKE

With size 6 (4mm) needles, cast on 64 sts.

1st row (wrong side) K to end.

2nd row K to end.

3rd and 4th rows P to end.

These 4 rows **form** the border patt and are repeated 3 times
more, so ending with a 4th row.

Now work in border and center panel patt as follows:

1st row (wrong side) K11, p42, k11.

2nd row K11, p42, k11.

3rd and 4th rows P to end.

These 4 rows **form** the main patt with border at each side, and
are repeated.

Work in patt as now set until work measures 23¼in/60cm,
ending with a 4th row.

Beg with a 1st row, work 16 rows in border patt across all sts.
Bind off purlwise.

TO FINISH

Cover one side of the buckram with fabric, folding in the excess.
Arrange two lengths of ribbon evenly spaced along the short
ends of the buckram and topstitch the fabric all around the
edges, catching the ribbons into the seam. Lay the wrong side
of the knitted piece on the uncovered side of the buckram and
slipstitch in place all around the edge. Tie the ribbons together
to create a tube, then lay your magazines inside.

Extra-Wide Cardigan

This fashionable slouch cardigan is perfect for every occasion and can be worn both at home and out and about. It is made in one of my most luxurious yarns, Baby Cashmerino. This is a fine-weight yarn with a cashmere blend, giving it a delightfully soft and comforting texture. It will take a little time to complete this cardigan so you will need to set aside some quiet me-time to make it, but your impressed family and friends will soon make it worth the effort.

MEASUREMENTS

To fit bust

32–34	36–38	40–42	44–46	in
81–86	92–97	102–107	112–117	cm

Finished measurements

Bust

51¼	55½	60¼	64½	in
130	141	153	164	cm

Length to shoulder

28¾	29¼	30¼	30¾	in
73	74.5	76.5	78	cm

Sleeve length

14¼in/36cm for all sizes

MATERIALS

* 14(15:16:17) 1¾ oz (50g) balls of Debbie Bliss Baby Cashmerino in Citrus 18
* Pair each of size 2 (3mm) and size 3 (3.25mm) knitting needles
* One size 2 (3mm) circular knitting needle
* 9 buttons

GAUGE

25 sts and 34 rows to 4in/10cm square over St st using size 3 (3.25mm) needles.

ABBREVIATIONS

See page 11.

BACK

With size 2 (3mm) needles, cast on 165(179:193:207) sts.

1st rib row K1, [p1, k1] to end.

2nd rib row P1, [k1, p1] to end.

Rep the last 2 rows 4 times more.

Change to size 3 (3.25mm) needles.

Beg with a k row, work in St st until back measures 15 ¾in/40cm from cast-on edge, ending with a p row.

Shape underarms and raglans

Bind off 5(7:9:11) sts at beg of next 2 rows. **155(165:175:185) sts.**

Next row K2, skp, k to last 4 sts, k2tog, k2.

Next row P to end.

Rep the last 2 rows 54(57:60:63) times more. **45(49:53:57) sts.**

Change to size 2 (3mm) needles.

1st rib row P1, [k1, p1] to end.

2nd rib row K1, [p1, k1] to end.

Rep the last 2 rows 3 times more.

Bind off in rib.

LEFT FRONT

With size 2 (3mm) needles, cast on 79(85:91:97) sts.

1st rib row P1, [k1, p1] to end.

2nd rib row K1, [p1, k1] to end.

Rep the last 2 rows 4 times more.

Change to size 3 (3.25mm) needles.

Beg with a k row, work in St st until front measures 15 ¾in/40cm from cast-on edge, ending with a p row.

Shape underarm, front neck, and raglan

1st row Bind off 5(7:9:11) sts, k to last 4 sts, k2tog, k2. **73(77:81:85) sts.**

Next row P to end.

Next row K2, skp, k to end.

Next row P2, p2tog, p to end.

Next row K2, skp, k to end.

Next row P to end.

Next row K2, skp, k to last 4 sts, k2tog, k2.

Next row P to end.

Rep the last 6 rows 6(6:7:7) times more. **38(42:41:45) sts.**

2nd and 4th sizes only

Next row K2, skp, k to end.

Next row P2, p2tog, p to end. –(40:–:43) sts.

All sizes

Next row K2, skp, k to end.

Next row P to end.

Rep the last 2 rows until 4 sts rem ending with a p row.

Leave these sts on a safety pin.

RIGHT FRONT

With size 2 (3mm) needles, cast on 79(85:91:97) sts.

1st rib row P1, [k1, p1] to end.

2nd rib row K1, [p1, k1] to end.

Rep the last 2 rows 4 times more.

Change to size 3 (3.25mm) needles.

Beg with a k row, work in St st until front measures 15 ¾in/40cm from cast-on edge, ending with a p row.

Shape underarm, front neck, and raglan

Next row K2, skp, k to end.

Next row Bind off 5(7:9:11) sts, p to end. **73(77:81:85) sts.**

Next row K to last 4 sts, k2tog, k2.

Next row P to last 4 sts, p2tog tbl, p2.

Next row K to last 4 sts, k2tog, k2.

Next row P to end.

Next row K2, skp, k to last 4 sts, k2tog, k2.

Next row P to end.

Rep the last 6 rows 6(6:7:7) times more. **38(42:41:45) sts.**

2nd and 4th sizes only

Next row K to last 4 sts, k2tog, k2.

Next row P to last 4 sts, p2tog tbl, p2. –(40:–:43) sts.

All sizes

Next row K to last 4 sts, k2tog, k2.

Next row P to end.

Rep the last 2 rows until 4 sts rem.

Leave these sts on a safety pin.

SLEEVES

With size 2 (3mm) needles, cast on 53(59:65:71) sts.

1st rib row P1, [k1, p1] to end.

2nd rib row K1, [p1, k1] to end.

Rep the last 2 rows 4 times more.

Change to size 3 (3.25mm) needles.

Beg with a k row, work in St st.

Work 8 rows.

Inc row K3, M1, k to last 3 sts, M1, k3.

Work 5 rows.

Rep the last 6 rows 13(14:15:16) times more and the inc row again. **83(91:99:107) sts.**

Work even until sleeve measures 14¼in/36cm from cast-on edge, ending with a p row.

Shape raglans

Bind off 5(7:9:11) sts at beg of next 2 rows. **73(77:81:85) sts.**

Next row K to end.

Next row P to end.

Next row K2, skp, k to last 4 sts, k2tog, k2.

Next row P to end.

Rep the last 4 rows 23(25:27:29) times more. **25(25:25:25) sts.**

Next row (right side) K2, skp, k to last 4 sts, k2tog, k2.

Next row P to end.

Rep the last 2 rows until 11(13:15:17) sts rem, ending with a p row. Leave these sts on a holder.

POCKETS (make 2)

With size 3 (3.25mm) needles, cast on 45(49:53:57) sts.

Beg with a k row, work 50(52:54:56) rows in St st.

Change to size 2 (3mm) needles.

1st rib row P1, [k1, p1] to end.

2nd rib row K1, [p1, k1] to end.

Rep the last 2 rows twice more.

Bind off in rib.

RIGHT FRONT AND NECK EDGING

With right side facing and size 2 (3mm) circular needle, pick up and k 100 sts up right front edge from cast-on edge to start of neck shaping, 89(93:97:101) sts up neck shaping to top of raglan, k 3 sts from safety pin, k last st tog with first st of right sleeve, then k rem 10(12:14:16) sts across right sleeve. 203(209:215:221) sts.

1st row P1, [k1, p1] to end.

2nd row P2, k1, [p1, k1] to end.

These 2 rows **form** the rib and are repeated.

Work 1 row more.

Buttonhole row (right side) Rib 3, yo, work 2tog, [rib 9, yo, work 2tog] 8 times, rib to end.

Rib 3 rows.

Bind off in rib.

LEFT FRONT AND NECK EDGING

With right side facing and size 2 (3mm) circular needle, k 10(12:14:16) sts across left sleeve, k last st tog with first st on safety pin of left front, k2, pick up and k 90(94:98:102) sts down left front neck, then 100 sts down left front edge to cast-on edge. 203(209:215:221) sts.

1st row P1, [k1, p1] to end.

2nd rib row K1, [p1, k1] to last 2 sts, p2.

These 2 rows **form** the rib.

Rep the last 2 rows twice more and the first row again.

Bind off in rib.

TO FINISH

Sew raglan and neckband seams. Sew on pockets. Sew side and sleeve seams. Sew on buttons.

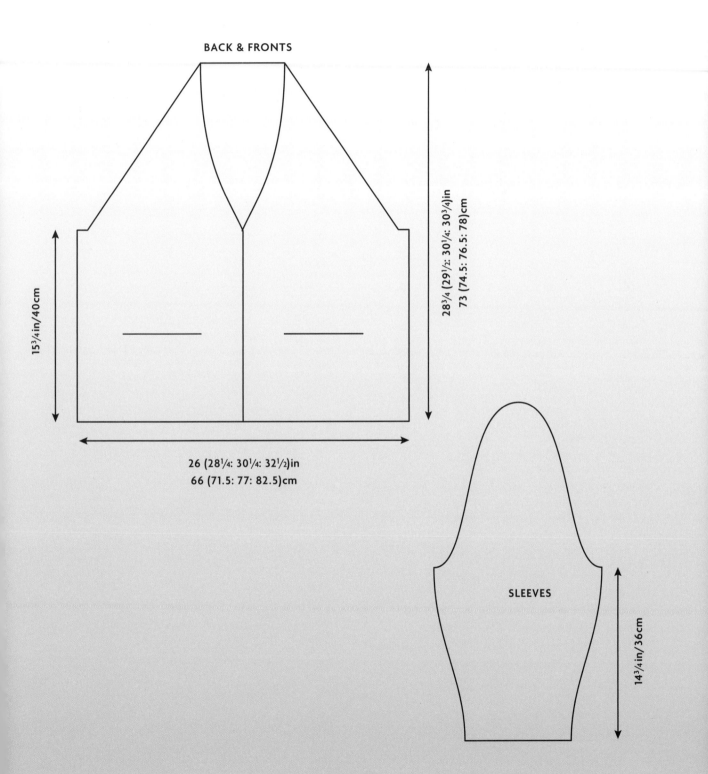

BACK & FRONTS

28³/₄ (29¹/₂: 30¹/₄: 30³/₄)in
73 (74.5: 76.5: 78)cm

15³/₄in/40cm

26 (28¹/₄: 30¹/₄: 32¹/₂)in
66 (71.5: 77: 82.5)cm

SLEEVES

14³/₄in/36cm

Hanging Pockets

If you find you are always short of storage space then this will prove the perfect method for de-cluttering your house. All that these hanging pockets need is a hook, so they can be placed on the back of a door or even on a wall. They are made using a double-knitting-weight cotton yarn, that will ensure a durable, sturdy knit that is perfect at keeping its shape even when it is holding objects of varying sizes and weights.

SIZE
Approximately 12¼in x 26in/31cm x 66cm

MATERIALS
✳ Five 1¾oz (50g) balls of Debbie Bliss Cotton DK in Mink 52 (A) and one ball in each of Duck Egg 09 (B), and Avocado 20 (C)
✳ Pair each of size 5 (3.75mm) and size 6 (4mm) knitting needles
✳ Piece of fabric for lining, 14¼in x 28in/36cm x 71cm
✳ Piece of heavyweight, stiff buckram, 12¼in x 26in/31cm x 66cm
✳ Sewing thread
✳ 17in/43cm length of wooden dowel to fit through the hanging loops

GAUGE
20 sts and 28 rows to 4in/10cm square over St st using size 6 (4mm) needles.

ABBREVIATIONS
See page 11.

TO MAKE

Lower pocket

** With size 5 (3.75mm) needles and A, cast on 63 sts.

Seed st row K1, [p1, k1] to end.

Rep this row 3 times more.

Change to size 6 (4mm) needles and work in patt as follows:

1st patt row (right side) [K1, p1] twice, k to last 4 sts, [p1, k1] twice.

2nd patt row K1, p1, k1, p to last 3 sts, k1, p1, k1.

These 2 rows **form** the main patt and are repeated.

Patt 2 rows.

Dec row [K1, p1] twice, ssk, k to last 6 sts, k2tog, [p1, k1] twice. **61 sts.**

Beg with a 2nd row, work 13 rows in patt.

Dec row [K1, p1] twice, ssk, k to last 6 sts, k2tog, [p1, k1] twice. **59 sts.**

Beg with a 2nd row, work 21 rows in patt.

Work 4 rows in seed st. **

Foldline row (right side) P to end.

Backing

*** Next row K1, p1, k1, p to last 3 sts, k1, p1, k1.

Next row [K1, p1] twice, k to last 4 sts, [p1, k1] twice.

Rep the last 2 rows until piece measures 25½in/65cm from ***, ending with a wrong-side row.

Now work 4 rows in seed st across all sts, so ending with a wrong-side row.

Hanging loops

Next row Seed st 13 sts, * bind off next 10 sts in seed st, with one st on needle after bind-off, seed st the next 12 sts; rep from * once more.

Working on the last group of 13 sts and leaving rem 2 groups of sts on the needle, seed st 27 rows, then bind off these 13 sts in seed st.

**** With wrong side facing, rejoin yarn to next group of 13 sts, work 27 rows in seed st, then bind off in seed st.

Rep from **** for last group of 13 sts.

MIDDLE POCKET

Work as Lower Pocket from ** to **, using B.

Bind off in seed st.

TOP POCKET

Work as Lower Pocket from ** to **, using C.

Bind off in seed st.

TO FINISH

Fold lower pocket onto right side of backing, along foldline. Sew pocket to backing along side edges. Arrange middle and top pockets evenly spaced on the backing and sew pocket sides and lower edge to backing, making sure that the cast-on edge forms the top edge of the pockets. Fold each hanging loop in half and sew the bound-off edge to the wrong side of the seed st top edge.

With sewing thread, hand stitch vertical lines through the backing and pockets to divide in sections.

Lining

Lay the lining fabric on the buckram, then fold and tape the excess onto the wrong side. Topstitch around the outside edge to keep the fabric in place. Hand sew the knitted piece to the covered buckram around the edges.

Indulge

Beaded Pillow

This stunning beaded pillow is pure indulgence. Perfect for adding a little luxury to every sofa and bed, it cannot fail to impress. I have knitted the pillow in a charming pale lilac and have decorated it in complementary colors with delicate ribbon and a complex bead detail. Although this may appear a slightly daunting knit, it is, in fact, made in manageable stages, and the ribbon and bead elements are only stitched at the end once the knitting of the pillow is complete.

SIZE
Approximately 12in x 16in/30cm x 40cm.

MATERIALS
✷ Four 1 ¾ oz (50g) balls of Debbie Bliss Baby Cashmerino in pale Lilac
✷ Pair of size 3 (3.25mm) knitting needles
✷ Approximately 25g of small glass embroidery beads—small purple glass beads, size SB07 color 8
✷ 13in/33cm lengths of assorted widths of ribbon, we used ¼in/7mm, ⅝in/15mm, and ¾in/2cm wide ribbons
✷ Sewing threads to match ribbons and sewing needle
✷ Pillow form to fit finished cover

ABBREVIATIONS
See page 11.

GAUGE
25 sts and 34 rows to 4in/10cm square over St st using size 3 (3.25mm) needles.

NOTE
✷ The cover is worked in one piece from the back opening, across the front and ending with the flap that will tuck in.
✷ If you use different width ribbons placed differently, you will need to adjust the instructions, but your cover front needs to be the same length as the back.
✷ When working St st channels between ridge rows, you need to work 3 rows for ¼in/7mm ribbon, 6 rows for ⅝in/15mm ribbon, and 8 rows for ¾in/2cm ribbon.

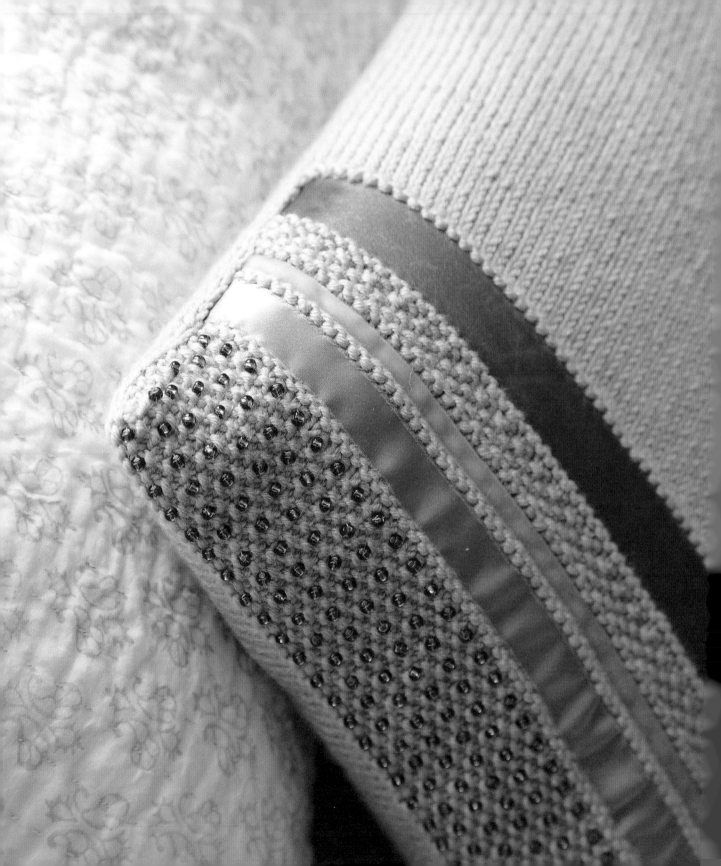

TO MAKE

The cover is worked in one piece.

Back

With size 3 (3.25mm) needles, cast on 77 sts.

Seed st row K1, [p1, k1] to end.

Rep this row 7 times more.

Beg with a k row, work in St st until piece measures 15¾in/40cm from cast-on edge, ending with a k row.

Foldline row (wrong side) K to end.

Front

Work 17 rows in seed st.

Ridge row (wrong side) K to end.

Beg with a k row, work 6 rows in St st, so ending with a p row.

Ridge row (right side) P to end.

Beg with a p row, work 3 rows in St st, so ending with a p row.

Ridge row (right side) P to end.

Work 4 rows in seed st.

Ridge row (wrong side) K to end.

Beg with a k row, work 8 rows in St st, so ending with a p row.

Ridge row (right side) P to end.

Beg with a p row, work in St st until piece measures 11½in/29cm from foldline row, ending with a k row.

Ridge row (wrong side) K to end.

Work 4 rows in seed st.

Ridge row (right side) P to end.

Beg with a p row, work 3 rows in St st, so ending with a p row.

Ridge row (right side) P to end.

Beg with a p row, work 6 rows in St st, so ending with a k row.

Ridge row (wrong side) K to end.

Beg with a k row, work 8 rows in St st, so ending with a p row.

Ridge row (right side) P to end.

Work in seed st until front measures 15¾in/40cm from foldline, ending with a k row.

Ridge row (wrong side) K to end.

Flap

Next row (right side) [K1, p1] 3 times, k to last 6 sts, [p1, k1] 3 times.

Next row K1, [p1, k1] twice, p to last 5 sts, [k1, p1] twice, k1.

Rep the last 2 rows until flap measures 4¾in/12cm from last foldline, ending with a wrong-side row.

Now work 8 rows in seed st across all sts.

Bind off in seed st.

TO DECORATE AND FINISH

Working on the pillow front only, sew beads to the seed st sections, sewing a bead under alternate purl stitches. Make sure beads are secure, but do not pull the thread too tightly or it will distort the finished pillow. Slipstitch the ribbons in place to the St st channels. Fold cover along the first foldline (between the back and front) and sew side seams from fold to cast-on edge (start of flap). Insert pillow form and tuck in flap.

Watchbands

Here is a way of brightening your wardrobe with a minimum amount of effort. Ideal for beginners, these are simple and fun knitting projects that can be made in a variety of color combinations and to your personal specifications. Each watchband only uses a small amount of yarn, so they are perfect for using up the leftover yarns that are undoubtably hanging around the bottom of your knitting bag.

SIZE

Seed stitch strap Approximately
⅝in x 20in/1.5cm x 51cm
Garter stitch strap Approximately
¾in x 19¾in/2cm x 50cm

MATERIALS

Seed stitch strap
* One 1¾ oz (50g) ball of Debbie Bliss Eco Baby in Blush 27
* Pair of size 3 (3mm) knitting needles

Garter stitch strap
* One 1¾ oz (50g) ball of Debbie Bliss Eco Baby in each of three colors—Ecru 16, Mint Green 20 (or Mauve 21), and Rose 12 (or Blush 27)
* Pair of 3mm (US 2-3) knitting needles

GAUGE

27 sts and 50 rows over seed st and 26 sts and 45 rows over garter st, both to 4in/10cm square using size 3 (3mm) needles.

ABBREVIATIONS

See page 11.

SEED ST STRAP

With size 3 (3mm) needles, using the thumb cast-on method
and Blush, cast on 139 sts.
Seed st row K1, [p1, k1] to end.
Rep this row 3 times more.
Bind off in seed st.

GARTER STITCH STRAP

With size 3 (3mm) needles, using the thumb cast-on method
and Mint Green (or Mauve), cast on 130 sts and k 2 rows.
K 2 rows in Ecru.
K 2 rows in Rose (or Blush).
K 2 rows in Ecru.
K 2 rows in Mint Green (or Mauve).
Bind off with Mint Green (or Mauve).

TO FINISH

Darn in yarn ends. Attach watch to band and tie around wrist.

Shrug

This delicate, show-stopping long line shrug in a gorgeous shade of pastel pink is one of the prettiest items in this book. Perfectly suited to be worn at home or to a party, this shrug looks stunning when paired with a graceful floaty dress. The shape of the shrug, with its simple lines and rolled edges, is soft and flattering on your body, while the fabric created by the beautiful mohair yarn is light and supple, ensuring that the outfit underneath is partially revealed and not drowned in weighty yarn.

MEASUREMENTS

To fit bust

32–34	36–38	40–42	44–46	48–50	in
81–86	92–97	102–107	112–117	122–127	cm

Finished measurements

Cuff to cuff

48 3/4	51	53 1/2	56	58 1/4	in
124	130	136	142	148	cm

Length to shoulder

29 1/2	30 1/4	30 3/4	31	31 3/4	in
75	76.5	78	79	80.5	cm

MATERIALS

✳ 6 (7: 8: 8: 9) 25g balls of Debbie Bliss Party Angel in Rose 19
✳ One long size 6 (4mm) circular knitting needle

GAUGE

22 sts and 30 rows to 4in/10cm square over St st using size 6 (4mm) needles.

ABBREVIATIONS

See page 11.

BACK

With size 6 (4mm) circular needle, cast on 88(98:108:118:128) sts.

Beg with a k row, work in St st backward and forward in rows throughout.

Work 12 rows.

Inc row K4, M1, k to last 4 sts, M1, k4.

Work 3 rows.

Rep the last 4 rows 28 times more. **146(156:166:176:186) sts.**

Shape sleeve

Cast on 2 sts at beg of next 44(46:48:50:52) rows.
234(248:262:276:290) sts.

Work even for 36(38:40:42:44) rows.

Shape upper arm

Bind off 7 sts at beg of next 10 rows and 7(8:9:10:11) sts at beg of next 8 rows. **108(114:120:126:132) sts.**

Shape shoulder

Bind off 14(15:16:17:18) sts at beg of next 4 rows.
52(54:56:58:60) sts.

K 1 row.

Bind off.

LEFT FRONT

With size 6 (4mm) circular needle, cast on 15(21:27:33:39) sts.

Beg with a k row, work in St st backward and forward in rows throughout.

Work 2 rows.

Shape front edge

Next row K to last st, M1, k1.

Next row P to end.

Rep the last 2 rows 4 times more. **20(26:32:38:44) sts.**

Inc row K4, M1, k to last st, M1, k1.

Next row P to end.

Next row K to last st, M1, k1.

Next row P to end.

Rep the last 4 rows 11 times more. **56(62:68:74:80) sts.**

This completes the front edge shaping

Inc row K4, M1, k to end.

Work 3 rows.

Rep the last 4 rows 16 times more. **73(79:85:91:97) sts.**

Shape sleeve

Next row Cast on 2 sts, k to end.

Next row P to end.

Rep the last 2 rows 21(22:23:24:25) times more.
117(125:133:141:149) sts.

Work even for 36(38:40:42:44) rows.

Shape upper arm

Bind off 7 sts at beg of next row and 4 foll right-side rows, then 7(8:9:10:11) sts at beg of 4 foll right-side rows. **54(58:62:66:70) sts.**

Shape shoulder

Next row P1, [p2tog] 26(28:30:32:34) times, p1.
28(30:32:34:36) sts.

Next row Bind off 14(15:16:17:18) sts, k to end.

Next row P to end.

Bind off rem 14(15:16:17:18) sts.

RIGHT FRONT

With size 6 (4mm) circular needle, cast on 15(21:27:33:39) sts.

Beg with a k row, work in St st backward and forward in rows throughout.

Work 2 rows.

Shape front edge

Next row K1, M1, k to end.

Next row P to end.

Rep the last 2 rows 4 times more. **20(26:32:38:44) sts.**

Inc row K1, M1, k to last 4 sts, M1, k4.

Next row P to end.

Next row K1, M1, k to end.

Next row P to end.

Rep the last 4 rows 11 times more. **56(62:68:74:80) sts.**

This completes the front edge shaping.

Inc row K to last 4 sts, M1, k4.

Work 3 rows.

Rep the last 4 rows 16 times more. **73(79:85:91:97) sts.**

Shape sleeve

Next row K to end.

Next row Cast on 2 sts, p to end.

Rep the last 2 rows 21(22:23:24:25) times more. **117(125:133:141:149) sts.**

Work even for 37(39:41:43:45) rows.

Shape upper arm

Bind off 7 sts at beg of next row and 4 foll wrong-side rows, then 7(8:9:10:11) sts at beg of 4 foll wrong-side rows. **54(58:62:66:70) sts.**

Shape shoulder

Next row K1, [k2tog] 26(28:30:32:34) times, k1. **28(30:32:34:36) sts.**

Next row Bind off 14(15:16:17:18) sts, p to end.

Next row K to end.

Bind off rem 14(15:16:17:18) sts.

CUFFS

Sew upper arm and shoulder seams.

With right side facing and size 6 (4mm) needles, pick up and k 54(57:60:63:66) sts along row-end edges at end of sleeve.

K 2 rows.

Bind off.

RIGHT FRONT EDGING

With right side facing and size 6 (4mm) needles, pick up and k 42 sts along shaped right front edge and 130(134:138:142:146) sts up front edge. **172(176:180:184:188) sts.**

Bind off.

LEFT FRONT EDGING

With right side facing and size 6 (4mm) needles, pick up and k 130(134:138:142:146) sts down left front edge and 42 sts along shaped edge. **172(176:180:184:188) sts.**

Bind off.

TO FINISH

Sew side and underarm seams.

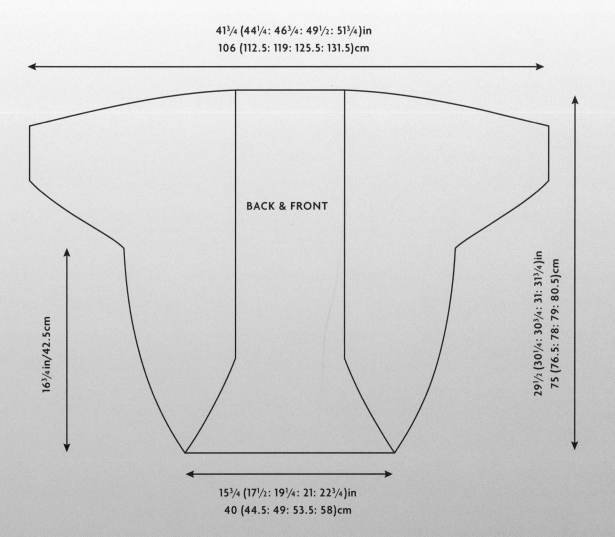

41¾ (44¼: 46¾: 49½: 51¾)in
106 (112.5: 119: 125.5: 131.5)cm

BACK & FRONT

29½ (30¼: 30¾: 31: 31¾)in
75 (76.5: 78: 79: 80.5)cm

16¾in/42.5cm

15¾ (17½: 19¼: 21: 22¾)in
40 (44.5: 49: 53.5: 58)cm

Keepsake Box

Here is an ingenious keepsake box that is suitable for storing your most treasured items. Create a pleasing background to enhance all your precious items that would otherwise be kept out of sight and collecting dust. This delightful pattern will brighten any room and can be made up in a variety of colors, whatever best suits your keepsake. So not only will you keep your item safe, you will also be presenting it in pride of place.

SIZE
Approximately 10in x 10in/25cm x 25cm.

MATERIALS
✱ Two 1 ¾ oz (50g) balls of Debbie Bliss Baby Cashmerino in Silver 12 (A) and one 1 ¾ oz (50g) ball in each of Ruby 700 (B), Baby Pink 601 (C), Ecru 101 (D), Indigo 207 (E), and Baby Blue 204 (F), plus small amount of Apple 02 (G)
✱ Pair of size 3 (3.25mm) knitting needles
✱ Box frame—Shadow box picture frame in white
✱ Narrow strip of pine molding for outer frame edge, and paints and gilding materials to decorate it

GAUGE
28 sts and 31 rows to 4in/10cm square over patterned St st using size 3 (3.25mm) needles.

ABBREVIATIONS
See page 11.

KEY FOR OVERLEAF
☐ Silver 12
◼ Ruby 700
☐ Baby Pink 601
☐ Ecru 101
☐ Baby Blue 204
◼ Indigo 207
☐ Apple 02

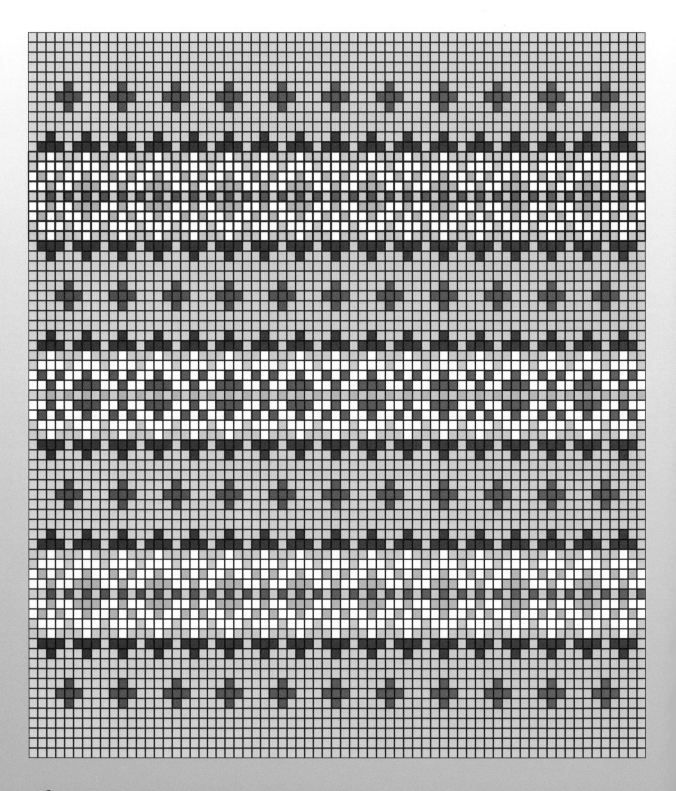

INDULGE

TO MAKE

With size 3 (3.25mm) needles and A, cast on 69 sts.

Beg with a k row, work 5 rows in St st.

Foldline row (wrong side) K to end.

Beg with a k row, work 73 rows in St st from chart, so ending with a k row.

Cont with A only.

Foldline row (wrong side) K to end.

Beg with a k row, work 5 rows in St st.

Bind off.

FRAME MOLDING

Using the strip of decorative pine molding, make a frame the same size as the box. Paint the frame to your color scheme using sample pots. We painted ours with light gray paint, then painted over this with a slightly pink off-white. We then distressed the frame by lightly sandpapering the painted surfaces, to show the under paint and wood in places. We applied silver-colored metal leaf in places using gilding size.

TO COMPLETE

Remove the backboard, mount, and glass from the box frame. Cut a piece of foamboard or cardboard slightly smaller than the inside of the box and stretch the knitted piece over the board, folding the excess over onto the back of the board, and secure in place with glue or tape—the foldline rows at the top and bottom will help. Attach your mementos to the covered board; if they are light enough, you could use the hook side of hook-and-loop tape, then slip inside the box. Attach the distressed frame to the box with double-sided tape. Depending on the depth of your mementos, you can either replace the glass in the frame or leave it out.

Headband

This is an exceptionally easy project to make, yet it is effective and comforting. This knit is also quick to make and takes only a single ball of Cashmerino Aran yarn to complete. Because it is knitted in two separate strips and then joined together at the end, even the most inexperienced knitter will immediately succeed with this headband. Suited for when you are lounging around the house, you will find yourself wearing this cute headband morning, noon, and night.

SIZE
Approximately 4¼in/11cm wide.

MATERIALS
✱ One 1¾ oz (50g) ball of Debbie Bliss Cashmerino Aran in Plum 17
✱ Pair of size 7 (4.5mm) knitting needles

GAUGE
21 sts and 34 rows to 4in/10cm square over seed st using size 7 (4.5mm) needles.

ABBREVIATIONS
See page 11.

MAIN BAND

With size 7 (4.5mm) needles, cast on 23 sts.
Seed st row K1, [p1, k1] to end.
Rep this row throughout.
Work in seed st until piece measures approximately 18in/46cm from cast-on edge.
Bind off in seed st.
Sew cast-on edge to bound-off edge.

CENTER BAND

With size 7 (4.5mm) needles, cast on 11 sts.
Beg with a k row, work in St st until piece measures approximately 5in/13cm or until just enough yarn to work the bind-off row remains.
Bind off.

TO FINISH

Wrap center band around main band and sew cast-on edge to bound-off edge. Move center band to sit around seam of main band.

Lace Collar

Fashionable and eye-catching, this graceful collar is a statement piece. Here I have used a subtle pale lilac, but choose a bold, vibrant color if you want to make your outfit even more striking. The best way to enliven any dress or make a plain top special is by wearing one of these peeking over the top. Made from only one ball of Rialto Lace, the collar can be made in a relatively short amount of time. It is ensured to turn heads, and there is no reason why you shouldn't knit yourself one or two!

SIZE

Approximately 4in/10cm at widest point x 24 1/2 in/62cm around lower edge.

MATERIALS

✳ One 1 ¾ oz (50g) ball of Debbie Bliss Rialto Lace in Lilac 11
✳ Pair of size 5 (3.75mm) knitting needles

GAUGE

28 sts and 35 rows to 4in/10cm square over patt using size 5 (3.75mm) needles.

ABBREVIATIONS

s2togkp = slip next 2 sts together as if to k2tog, k1, pass 2 sts over.
Also see page 11.

TO MAKE

With size 5 (3.75mm) needles, cast on 175 sts.

K 1 row.

Now work in patt as follows:

1st row (right side) K3, [yo, k3, s2togkp, k3, yo, k1] to last 2 sts, k2.

2nd and every foll wrong-side row K3, p to last 3 sts, k3.

3rd row K3, [k1, yo, k2, s2togkp, k2, yo, k2] to last 2 sts, k2.

5th row K3, [k2, yo, k1, s2togkp, k1, yo, k3] to last 2 sts, k2.

7th row K3, [k3, yo, s2togkp, yo, k4] to last 2 sts, k2.

8th row K3, p to last 3 sts, k3.

Rep the last 8 rows 3 times more.

Next row K3, [k3, s2togkp, k4] to last 2 sts, k2. **141 sts.**

K 1 row.

Next row K5, [k2tog, k6] to end. **124 sts.**

Bind off knitwise.

TO FINISH

Make two twisted cords each approximately 15in/38cm long
and attach one to each end of bound-off edge, knotting the
ends to prevent unraveling. Pin collar out to size and block
to shape.

Chevron Pillow

Add a quirky, yet elegant touch to your room with this startling chevron pillow. This zig-zag design is a classic and is, suprisingly, easier to achieve than it looks. The design is reflected in the edging of the pillow and accented by the simple button detail. It is worth knitting this in bold and unusual color combinations as the pattern will make more of an impact. But you can, of course, knit this in much paler shades if you desire a more subtle effect.

SIZE
Approximately 14in/35cm square.

MATERIALS
✱ Two 1 ¾ oz (50g) balls of Debbie Bliss Baby Cashmerino in Sienna 67 (M) and one ball in each of Lilac Pink 69 (A), Pale Lilac 608 (B) White 100 (C), and Peach Melba 68 (D)
✱ Pair of size 3 (3.25mm) knitting needles
✱ 7 buttons
✱ Pillow form to fit finished cover

GAUGE
25 sts and 34 rows to 4in/10cm square over St st using size 3 (3.25mm) needles.

ABBREVIATIONS
p2sso = pass 2 slipped sts over.
Also see page 11.

TO MAKE

With size 3 (3.25mm) needles and A, cast on 101 sts.

1st (buttonhole) row (right side) K14, [yo, k2tog, k10] to last 15 sts, yo, k2tog, k13.

2nd row P to end.

Now work in patt and stripe sequence as follows:

Work 2 rows in each of B, C, M, D, and A.

1st row (right side) K2, skp, * k9, sl 2, k1, p2sso; rep from * to last 13 sts, k9, k2tog, k2. **85 sts.**

2nd row P7, * [p1, yo, p1] in next st, p9; rep from * to last 8 sts, [p1, yo, p1] in next st, p7. **101 sts.**

Cont in patt until work measures 12in/30cm from cast-on edge, ending with a 1st row in M. **85 sts.**

Cont in M only.

Foldline row (wrong side) K to end.

Beg with a **k row**, work 13 1/2in/34cm more in St st, ending with a k row.

Foldline row (wrong side) K to end.

Beg with a **k row**, work 4in/10cm more in St st, ending with a k row.

K 2 rows.

Bind off.

TO FINISH

Fold piece along foldlines and sew side seams. Insert pillow form. Sew on buttons.

Lacy Shawl

With its gently scalloped triangular shape, this exquisite wrap shawl sits weightlessly across the shoulders and drapes downward to a point at the center back. It is the perfect showcase for the breathtakingly beautiful fern lace stitch, which is actually deceptively easy to knit. In this delicate lilac shade, the lacy shawl is so elegant it could be just as easily worn for an evening event as around the home.

SIZE
One size approximately 83 1/2 in/212cm wide x 44in/112cm deep.

MATERIALS
* Five 7/8 oz (25g) balls of Debbie Bliss Angel in Lilac 18
* One long size 8 (5mm) circular knitting needle
* Pair of size 8 (5mm) knitting needles

GAUGE
17 sts and 13 rows to 4in/10cm square over patt using size 8 (5mm) needles.

ABBREVIATIONS
sk2togp = slip 1, k2tog, pass slipped st over. Also see page 11.

TO MAKE

With size 8 (5mm) circular needle, cast on 361 sts.

Work backward and forward in rows.

K 3 rows.

Now work in patt as follows:

1st row K4, skp, k3, [sk2togp, k3, yo, k1, yo, k3] to last 12 sts, sk2togp, k3, k2tog, k4.

2nd, 4th, 6th, and 8th rows K3, p to last 3 sts, k3.

3rd row K7, [sk2togp, k2, yo, k3, yo, k2] to last 10 sts, sk2togp, k7.

5th row K6, [sk2togp, k1, yo, k5, yo, k1] to last 9 sts, sk2togp, k6.

7th row K5, [sk2togp, yo, k7, yo] to last 8 sts, sk2togp, k5.

These 8 rows **form** the patt and are repeated.

Cont in patt until 21 sts rem, ending with a wrong-side row and changing to size 8 (5mm) straight needles when appropriate.

Next row (right side) K4, skp, k3, sk2togp, k3, k2tog, k4.

2nd, 4th, 6th, and 8th rows K3, p to last 3 sts, k3.

3rd row K7, sk2togp, k7.

5th row K6, sk2togp, k6.

7th row K5, sk2togp, k5.

Cont in this way until 3 sts rem.

K3tog and fasten off.

YARN DISTRIBUTORS

For stockists of Debbie Bliss yarns please contact:

USA
Knitting Fever Inc.
315 Bayview Avenue
Amityville,
NY 11701
USA
Tel: +1 516 546 3600
Fax +1 516 546 6871
www.knittingfever.com

UK & WORLDWIDE DISTRIBUTORS
Designer Yarns Ltd
Units 8-10 Newbridge Industrial Estate
Pitt Street, Keighley
W. Yorkshire BD21 4PQ
UK
Tel: +44 (0)1535 664222
Fax: +44 (0)1535 664333
e-mail: enquiries@designeryarns.uk.com
www.designeryarns.uk.com

CANADA
Diamond Yarn Ltd
155 Martin Ross Avenue,
Unit 3,
Toronto
Ontario M3J 2L9
Canada
Tel: +1 416 736 6111
Fax: +1 416 736 6112
www.diamondyarn.com

DENMARK
Fancy Knit
Storegade, 13
8500 Grenaa
Ramten
DENMARK

Tel: +45 86 39 88 30
Fax: +45 20 46 09 06
e-mail: Kelly@fancyknitdanmark.com

MEXICO
Estambres Crochet SA de CV
Aaron Saenz 1891-7
Col. Santa Maria
Monterrey
N.L. 64650
Mexico
Tel: +52 81 8335 3870
e-mail: abremer@redmundial.com.mx

ICELAND
Storkurinn ehf
Laugavegi 59
101 Reykjavík
ICELAND
Tel: +354 551 8258
Fax: +354 562 8252
e-mail: storkurinn@simnet.is

GERMANY/AUSTRIA/SWITZERLAND/ BENELUX
Designer Yarns (Deutschland) GmbH
Welserstrasse 10g
D-51149 Köln
GERMANY
Tel: +49 (0) 2203 1021910
Fax: +49 (0) 2203 1023551
e-mail: info@designeryarns.de
www.designeryarns.de

FRANCE
PLASSARD DIFFUSION
La Filature,
71800 Varennes-sous-Dun
FRANCE
Tel: +33 (0) 3 85282828
Fax: +33 (0) 3 85282829
e-mail: info@laines-plassard.com

SPAIN
Oyambre Needlework SL
Balmes, 200 At.4
08006 Barcelona
SPAIN
Tel: +34 (0) 93 487 26 72
Fax: +34 (0) 93 218 6694
e-mail: info@oyambreonline.com

SWEDEN
Nysta garn och textil
Hogasvagen 20
S-131 47 Nacka
Tel: +46 (0) 708 813 954
e-mail: info@nysta.se
www.nysta.se

AUSTRALIA/NEW ZEALAND
Prestige Yarns Pty Ltd
Unit 6
8-10 Pioneer Drive
Bellambi NSW 2517
AUSTRALIA
Tel: +61 02 4285 6669
e-mail: info@prestigeyarns.com
www.prestigeyarns.com

FINLAND
Eiran Tukku
Mäkelänkatu 54 B
00510 Helsinki
FINLAND
Tel: +358 50 346 0575
e-mail: maria.hellbom@eirantukku.fi

BRAZIL
Quatro Estacoes Com
Las Linhas e Acessorios Ltda
Av. Das Nacoes Unidas
12551-9 Andar
Cep 04578-000 Sao Paulo
BRAZIL

Tel: +55 11 3443 7736
e-mail: cristina@4estacoeslas.com.br

TAIWAN
U-Knit
1F,
199-1 Sec,
Zhong Xiao East Road,
Taipei,
Tel: + 886 2 27527557
Fax: +886 2 27528556
e-mail: shuindigo@hotmail.com

RUSSIA
Golden Fleece Ltd
Soloviyny proezd 16,
117593 Moscow
Russian Federation
Tel: +8 (903) 000-1967
e-mail: natalya@rukodelie.ru
www.rukodelie.ru

THAILAND
Needle World Co Ltd
Pradit Manoontham Road,
Bangkok 10310
Tel: 662 933 9167
Fax: 662 933 9110
e-mail: needle-world.coltd@
googlemail.com

HONG KONG
East Unity Company Ltd
Unit B2,
7/F Block B,
Kailey Industrial Centre,
12 Fung Yip Street,
Chan Wan
Tel: (852) 2869 7110
Fax: (852) 2537 6952
e-mail: eastunity@yahoo.com.hk

NORWAY
Viking of Norway
Bygdaveien 63
4333 Oltedal
Tel: +47 516 11 660
Fax: +47 516 16 235
e-mail: post@viking-garn.no
www.viking-garn.no

SOUTH KOREA
AnnKnitting
#1402 14F, Dongjin Bldg
735-6 Gyomun-dong, Guri-si
Gyeonggi-do
471-020 South Korea
Tel: +82 70 4367 2779
Fax: +82 2 6937 0577
e-mail: tedd@annknitting.com
www.annknitting.com

ITALY
Lucia Fornasari
Via Cuniberti, 22
Ivrea (TO)
10015
e-mail: luciafornasae@hotmail.it
www.lavoroamaglia.it

For more information on my other books
and yarns, please visit:
www.debbieblissonline.com

Editorial Director Jane O'Shea
Creative Director Helen Lewis
Commissioning Editor Lisa Pendreigh
Editor Louise McKeever
Designers Nicola Ellis and Ros Holder
Photographer Penny Wincer
Stylist Mia Pejcinovic
Production Director Vincent Smith
Production Controller Aysun Hughes

First published in the United States of America
in 2013 by
Trafalgar Square Books
North Pomfret, Vermont 05053

Printed in China

Originally published in the United Kingdom
in 2013 by
Quadrille Publishing Ltd, London

ISBN: 978 1 57076 605 3

Library of Congress Control Number:
2012952544